NeuroLeadership

How The *World's Best Leaders* Use Psychology To Win

Felicia Page

NeuroLeadership:
How The World's Best Leaders
Use Psychology To Win

Copyright © 2017

All rights reserved to the author

No part of this book may be reproduced, scanned, or distributed in any manner whatsoever without written permission from the author except in the case of brief quotation embodied in critical articles and reviews with direct, immediate and clear reference to the author.

DISCLAIMER

Please note the information contained within this document is for educational purposes only.

Every attempt has been made to provide accurate, up to date and reliable complete information. No warranties of any kind are expressed or implied. Readers acknowledge that the author is not engaging in rendering legal, financial or professional advice. Readers should obtain professional advice where appropriate, where their specific content and situation can be taken into consideration, before making any such decisions.

By reading any document, the reader agrees that under no circumstances is the author responsible for any losses, direct or indirect, which are incurred as a result of use of the information contained within this document directly or indirectly, including not taking action based upon the information in this book – and not limited to errors, omissions, or inaccuracies"

Table of Contents

Preface	1
1. The Psychology of Decision Making	5
2. Using Psychology to Build Credibility	17
3. Using Psychology to Influence and Persuade	29
4. The Psychology of Modesty and Humility in Leaders	41
5. The Psychology of Power	55
6. Using Psychology to Build Resilience	71
7. The Psychology of Emotional Intelligence	89
8. The Psychology of Motivation	105
9. How to Use Psychology to Enhance Goal Setting	123
10. How Psychology Can Help You Improve Productivity	141
11. Using Psychology to Recruit Top Talent	161
12. Using Psychology to Enhance Feedback	177
13. Using Psychology to Handle Conflict and Deal with Difficult People	193
14. The Psychology of Teams	207
15. Using Psychology to Influence Culture	221
16. The Psychology of Change	233
17. The Psychology of Millennials	247
Conclusion	263
Citations	265

Preface

Why write another leadership book? It's a good question, one I certainly grappled with before putting pen to paper. I knew this book had to be different from what was already out there, and interesting enough that you would actually read it.

I decided on addressing a gap—a gap between what science knows and how leaders act. See, science has discovered many things about people in the workplace; how output can be increased, happiness improved, patterns of communication optimized. But these research insights rarely make it outside the lab, and that's a gap I aim to bridge for you.

This book brings psychological research together with practical application. The science of leadership with its implementation. It is written for the entrepreneur, the CEO, the executive, and the senior manager. In short, for leaders in the real world, and not for academics.

For the most part, each chapter is written to be independent of the others, and does not have to be read sequentially. You can, of course, but you may also turn to any section which is of immediate interest and begin there. The reason for structuring the book like this is because leaders are some of the most time-poor people I know.

The benefit is you now have a resource you can turn to whenever you need to develop your hiring strategy, lead your people or organization through periods of change, build emotional intelligence, or any of the other 17 areas of leadership-psychology covered in this book. With this book, you can quickly get hold of evidenced-based, practical strategies and, should you wish to dig a little deeper, an extensive reference list is provided at the end of the book.

To strike a balance of fascination, rigor, and utility, each chapter has been broken into sections. Though not always in precise order, the sections are as follows:

1. **Opening quote**

    This is to set the frame for what is to come. The majority of quotes come from leaders of varying fields, not always business.

2. **Introduction to the topic**

    Providing context for what the chapter is about, this is an overview with definitions and/or examples.

3. **Why this topic is important**

    This section presents the case for the topic, discussing why it matters.

4. **Key research findings**

    Here, you will get a break down of the actual methodology and findings from the most relevant research on each topic. This research comes from the university departments of psychology, economics, sociology, and management. There is also a mix of recent and pioneering research.

5. **Case studies**

   Perhaps the most interesting to me, this section presents historical anecdotes which demonstrate how each topic has applied to varying situations. For example, how Walt Disney motivated his staff at Disneyland. Or, how U.S. President Jimmy Carter mediated the Israeli-Palestinian conflict.

6. **How you can apply these findings**

   The purpose of the research and case studies is to provide you with principles you may draw from and apply within your own organization or department. To aid this process, I've provided some explicit suggestions for application in each chapter.

7. **Chapter summary**

   A list of bullet points which recap the relevant concepts, research, and practical suggestions covered in the chapter.

I've learned a great deal putting this book together. My hope is that you will find it both immediately useful, and a great resource to return to later. Tear, scribble, dog-ear, underline.

Do as you must—these are the signs of a book well observed. Should your copy become too defaced, reach out and I will gladly provide you a second, on me.

1
The Psychology of Decision Making

Clearly, the decision-making that we rely on in society is fallible. It's highly fallible, and we should know that.
~ Daniel Kahneman

Ask any leader how they go about making an important decision, and you will likely hear some variation of this response: *I weigh all of my options carefully, apply logic, and choose the best option*. That's what every person wants to believe. Nobody wants to think that they're held hostage by things like emotion, fear, or cognitive biases.

Moreover, if you ask most leaders to rate their decision-making ability, they'll rate themselves highly. Just as when, if you ask a room full of people to raise their hand if they think they are an above average driver, the majority will. Of course, statistically, this is unlikely[1].

---

1   This is an example of the 'above average effect' where only a small number of people tend to rate themselves as below average, when in fact 50% should.

We also know from studies and real-world examples that leaders will rate their decision making as high-quality even when the decisions they make are reckless and ill-advised.

Let's look at one quick example. A 2012 study in the Wall Street Journal1 looked at the decisions made by leaders at Lehman Brothers prior to their bankruptcy. Lehman Brothers had borrowed money in order to invest in mortgage-backed securities and a variety of other investments. By the time the economy crashed, the company had borrowed 31 dollars for every one dollar of equity they had.

In hindsight, the decision to borrow so much seems foolhardy at best. To give them the benefit of the doubt, perhaps the leaders at Lehman Brothers felt they were giving the company an opportunity to grow. At the time, they were generating tremendous profits. However, it is now clear that they made poor decisions that directly contradicted not only the company's interest, but also their own. But they did it anyway. Why?

How our brains make decisions

In Nobel Prize winner Daniel Kahneman's book *Thinking, Fast and Slow*[2], he describes two basic kinds of decision making:

1. **System 1 thinking:** System 1 thinking is rapid and requires little conscious thought. The brain makes a series of quick assessments and judgments based

on things like body language, tone of voice, and an assortment of cognitive biases. Cognitive biases are mental shortcuts. Mental shortcuts can be useful in that they allow your brain to conserve energy. They also allow you to make split-second decisions—an evolutionary necessity if, for example, you run into a tiger and need to make the immediate decision to fight or flee. This is something we will talk more about later in the book.

2. **System 2 thinking**: System 1 thinking involves deep thought, cognitive assessments, and value comparisons. Unlike System 1 decisions, System 2 decisions tend to be carefully evaluated.

Most people believe that they use System 2 to make decisions, but the evidence doesn't support that conclusion. Not only does using System 2 require the decision maker to overcome pre-existing biases and misconceptions, it is also easily derailed.

Adhering to System 2 decision making requires attention. One classic example provided by Kahneman is that of a group of people who were asked to watch a video of a basketball game.[3] They were instructed to count the passes made by the players on one team while ignoring the other team. In the middle of the video, a woman in a gorilla costume walks slowly into the center of the court and dances – surely something that would be obvious to even the most casual observer. Yet over half of the people who viewed the video didn't see the gorilla. They had been told to ignore everything other than the white team's passes, and so their brains did.

Interestingly, once people were told about the gorilla in the video, they saw it every time from then on, even if they were shown a different version of the video. From that point forward, they could not not-see the gorilla.

Cognitive Biases

Cognitive biases are another example of System 1 thinking. Hundreds of cognitive biases have been discovered, including:

- **Status Quo Bias:** The role of the Status Quo Bias in decision making was studied in 1988 by researchers William Samuelson and Richard Zeckhauser.[4] Their study showed that, more often than not, participants would choose to stay with the status quo when presented with a new alternative. That preference held true when it came to politics (re-electing incumbents), employment (staying in their current job), and purchasing decisions (sticking with a familiar product.)

- **Sunk Cost Fallacy:** Robert Knox and James Inkster[5] examined bettors' confidence in bets they placed on a horse race, and found that those who had already placed their bets had a higher degree of confidence that they had made a good choice than those who had not yet placed their bets. In other words, when we have made a commitment to something and invested time, effort, and money, we're likely to double down on that investment. We do this even when evidence suggests that another course of action might be preferable.

- **Loss Aversion:** This is where we are more inclined to place a stronger focus on avoiding losses than acquiring gains. This is what makes people place a higher premium on things they already have than on things they might get at a later date.

One of the trickiest things about cognitive biases is that we're all susceptible to them. We tell ourselves that we base decisions on logic, but as Kahneman says in his book, unless something gives us pause—makes us switch from System 1 to System 2—we're likely making important decisions based on biases instead of brainwork.

So why does this matter?

Faulty decision-making processes wreak havoc within organizations. When listing qualities and skills that are important in leadership and management, most hiring professionals mention resilience and people skills, as well as specialized, industry-related skills, but decision making often does not even make it onto the list. That's unfortunate, because a leader who lacks the ability to make good decisions runs the risk of causing, or contributing to, big problems in their department or organization.

Let's look at an example. The Eastman Kodak Company had, in the 1970s, a 90% share of the film market in the United States. In 1975, they developed the first technology to make digital cameras, but they never acted on it because the leaders of the company feared that the new cameras would cut into their share of the film market. The lack of foresight in that decision is now viewed as remarkable, especially given what we now know about digital technology. It ultimately cost Kodak billions of dollars in digital camera sales and transformed the company.[6]

The Lesson of Kodak

Kodak is a great example of loss aversion. The question Kodak's story should make us ask is, as leaders, what can we do to avoid the same decision making errors as Kodak and similar companies?

Education is an important first step. But, don't be fooled into thinking that just knowing all of the cognitive biases will help you and your leaders make better decisions. What we know from the latest neuroscience studies is that simply knowing the cognitive bias does not stop your brain from using the cognitive bias.

Acceptance that everyone is susceptible is critical. Regardless of how cautious you are, there are cognitive biases that affect the way you think. Many of your leaders will not believe this, even when themselves tested by something like the gorilla video. Instead, you need to ensure that systems are in place so that the control is taken out of their hands. For example:

- Never allow a critical decision to be made by one person.
- Build a safe work environment where it is okay to identify and raise instances when biases might be influencing decision making.
- Promote a company-wide decision-making process like Toyota's '5 Whys' or 7-step problem solving strategy[7]
- Influence a culture of quality decision making by:
    - Rewarding people who learn from mistakes
    - Not accepting "gut feelings" or "gut decisions" for complex problems
    - Forming diverse teams to improve decision making
    - Giving people enough time when they are solving complex problems
    - Having a quality risk management process in place
    - Making your expectations and the vision clear

- Providing critical information quickly and openly
- Role-modeling quality decision making

How to Improve Your Decision-Making Skills

Chances are good that, as you read this chapter, you reflected on some previous decisions and saw areas where you were influenced by biases. Perhaps you even thought of a decision that resulted in a very poor outcome, similar to the one made by Kodak. Like everyone, you are susceptible to biases.

Some of the most effective strategies to combat bias that I have used with leaders include:

1. **Considering options independently first, and then comparing.** When you need to make a choice between options, there are two main approaches you can take:

    a. Compare the options against each other

    b. Assess each option individually and then pick the highest rated option

    For complex options, it is more effective to assess options independently first and then compare ratings. The reason for this is that, when you are faced with complex problems, the brain adopts simplifying strategies, like System 1 thinking, causing you to consider only a fraction of the available information. So, the best approach for complex options is to assess independently first to ensure that you are considering all available information.

For simple or less important decisions however, like what to have for lunch, comparing options is a smart strategy. With this approach, you will be able to make a quicker decision and there is less risk if you miss a piece of information.

2. **Valuing and asking for other people's input.** Just because you are paid the big bucks does not mean that you have to know everything. That is why you have people around you—to provide their expertise and different points of view. It is your job to determine which information to then act on. Be cautious about asking input from too many people. Determine whom to go to for what information.

3. **Putting yourself in another person's shoes.** Take a moment to imagine things from other people's perspectives. This will help you to expand your horizons and will also make it easier for you to overcome other people's objections once you have decided on a course of action.

4. **Checking how you are feeling.** Are you tired, are you angry? Is this the best time for you to be making this decision? If in the past you have made a decision or said something or sent an email that you regretted,

try next time to wait until you are calmer or more alert before making a decision. Most people are at their most alert in the morning. This will help you to make System 2 decisions that require high attention.

5. **Reducing stress**. Don't expect your brain to be creative when you are stressed or tired. When you are stressed or tired you brain will revert to System 1 thinking. You will be more prone to cognitive biases. You will be more inclined to focus on the positive aspects of your decision and pass over the negative elements. Stress will also impact your risk-taking appetite. Chapter 8 covers the psychology of resilience and practical tips for reducing stress.

6. **Evaluating the idea by asking:**
   a. Why are you doing this?
   b. What do you hope to achieve?
   c. What might be the negative consequences?
   d. Are you making any assumptions? (You need to verify your assumptions. Data is key. Validating that data is also key)
   e. Do you have any hesitations? If so, why? Do you have any emotional attachments?
   f. What is your plan?
   g. What are the risks?

h. What are the alternatives?

   i. Is this consistent with the mission, vision, what you have said previously, other initiatives in the organization, and your values?

7. **Conducting a cost/benefit analysis.**

8. **Anticipating the consequences of a decision.**

9. **Quickly taking ownership and responding with a backup plan if a decision goes wrong.**

Key Takeaways

1. Decision making is an essential skill for leaders.

2. System 1 decision making is quick and biased, involving very little logical thinking or rational analysis.

3. System 2 decision making is rational and methodical, but easily affected by a loss of attention.

4. Cognitive biases affect everybody, including leaders at every level. Understanding what they are and how they work can help you use them to your advantage.

5. Simple techniques such as asking questions that could be posed by a person with an alternative viewpoint, avoiding distractions, and putting yourself in the other person's shoes can help make your decision-making process more effective than it is now.

2

Using Psychology to Build Credibility

Credibility is the foundation of leadership.
~ James M. Kouzes and Barry Z. Posner

People who lack credibility can't be effective leaders. Leading a company and its employees is complicated. If your employees don't have confidence that you and other leaders in the organization know what you are doing, they are not going to be able to do their jobs efficiently. Instead, any doubt in leadership's credibility will set off a tidal wave of inefficiency and discontentment.[1]

What Is Credibility?

There are three primary criteria that influence the perception of a person as credible.[2]

1. The *perception* of whether the person has a vested interest in a particular outcome
2. The position advocated by the person

3. The person's similarity to those to whom they are speaking

In other words, credibility is about believability and trust. If a person believes that you are acting according to self-interests, are not knowledgeable in the position you are advocating, and/or share no common ground, then they are less likely to see you as credible.

When someone believes that you are credible, they trust that you have the knowledge to make appropriate decisions and the integrity to do things in a way that is proper.

Why does credibility matter?

Consider how credibility affects your response to people. If you bought a car from a dealer who misled you, how likely would you be to buy from them again? If you received financial advice from a person who did not appear knowledgeable in the advice they were giving, how likely would you be to take that advice?

When people let you down, mislead you, or give you information that you do not believe, they destroy their credibility. You would not give your trust to someone who had no credibility, nor should you expect your employees or stakeholders to do so.

In the workplace, when employees feel that their leader lacks credibility, they will question the leader's motives and abilities. They will experience discomfort at the thought of carrying out orders. Their morale and productivity will suffer. Even if employees end up following directives, the lack of trust and confidence impacts every area of their performance.

On the other hand, employees who believe strongly in their leader's credibility are more likely to carry out job duties quickly and efficiently, and with a high degree of confidence. They are also more likely to accept changes. For example, a 2000 study found that employees who felt their leaders had credibility were more likely to accept changes in the systems used to determine salaries.[3] They were also more likely to accept performance reviews they had been given.

Subordinates are not the only ones to whom credibility matters. A 2001 study examined the relationships between city administrators and municipal boards.[4] What it found was that, when leaders had credibility, they were able to nurture productive, open, and trust-based relationships with board members. Credible leaders were better able to encourage cooperation than leaders who lacked credibility.

The impact of credibility for Lululemon

In 2013, apparel company Lululemon ran into a serious credibility problem that went from bad to worse even after a change of leadership.[5] The problem started when customers complained that yoga pants sold by the company were too sheer, forcing the company to pull pants from store shelves and correct the manufacturing problem that led to the complaints. After this issue was resolved, the company's CEO, Christine Day, announced she was stepping down. Shares plummeted, and then a former employee publicly shamed the company by talking about their bad treatment of customers who wore larger sizes, stating that the management at her store openly discriminated against customers based on their weight.

The company's new CEO then made a statement saying that the company's pants weren't for every woman's body. Specific comments about "rubbing thighs" lent credence to the statements made by former employees and as a result this impacted the CEO's credibility—as well as the company's. The result was a drop in stock prices and a significant drop in customer confidence.[6]

As you can see, the problems that Lululemon encountered were not really a result of the manufacturing problem that led to the first customer complaints. Rather, they were a direct result of a series of actions that impacted the credibility of the company's leadership team and the company.

The psychological principles of credibility

There are a number of factors that influence credibility. Three key factors for a leader are how you deal with failure, manage self-interests, and present your message. Let's take a look.

- **Placing blame**. A 2001 social-psychology study looked at how the practice of placing blame for negative outcomes affected the perception of leaders.[7] What it found was that leaders who sought out others to blame for their failures were perceived by employees as lacking power and credibility. Conversely, leaders who accepted blame for their shortcomings gained credibility with their subordinates.

- **Arguing against your own self-interest**. The idea of arguing against your own self-interest is not a new one. The power of this idea was famously illustrated in the classic film Miracle on 34th Street. When the Santa Claus at Macy's started recommending products sold by other stores, the company's credibility with customers skyrocketed. While this is a fictional example from a movie, the premise holds true in the real world.

   The negative effects of playing to your self-interests are demonstrated in a 1999 study that showed that stockbrokers lost credibility when they made "buy" recommendations on stocks that their companies had recently taken public.[8] Not only did their personal credibility suffer as a result of their perceived self-interest, but the stocks underperformed as well.

- **Facts and figures**. Have you ever wondered why politicians tend to quote so many facts and statistics when they make speeches or engage in debates? It's because precise statements endow the person who makes them with credibility. This holds true even when the statements themselves are inaccurate.[9] Not only that, but the more specific the claims made, the more credible they seem. For example, a statement that 'more than half of all Americans support gun-control legislation' was viewed as much less credible than the more specific statement saying that '55.2% of Americans support stronger gun control legislation'. People viewed the second statement as more credible because it was more precise.

Practical Tools for improving your credibility

Being accountable for your shortcomings, precision, and arguing against your own self-interest are three principles that can do a lot to cement your reputation as a credible leader. It's not enough to demand credibility. Credibility is earned and the only way to do that is to behave in a way that makes your employees and stakeholders trust and respect you.

There are many things that you can do to increase your credibility. I have included below a number of practical tools that I have seen work for many leaders in many different situations. But first note, if you are not currently viewed as credible, it is going to take time to reverse this negative perception. Making drastic changes that are very different to your norm will only put people off because they will question your motivation. Building credibility is all about genuine trust and this requires incremental change.

- **Accept responsibility when things go wrong.** Placing blame on others is very easy, especially when the other parties are not in the room. But this is one of the key sacrifices of leadership—taking the blame when things go wrong and giving praise to others when it goes right. While it may hurt at the time, taking the blame for something that may have been caused by one of your subordinates will help you in the long run. Employees will respect you for being willing to admit shortcomings—and they'll be more likely to trust you in the future.

- **Argue against your own self-interest.** How can you translate this idea to your workplace? Most people have a strong sense of self-preservation. Perhaps the most effective way to increase credibility is to play devil's advocate in situations where you have a lot to gain. If employees perceive that your primary interest is helping yourself, they will not see you as credible. However, if you make a point of openly arguing the other side of the issue, your employees will perceive you to be a fair and effective leader—and they'll see you as being a credible source of information and guidance even if your ultimate decision results in a net gain for you.

- **Work as much for your employees as they work for you.** Do you think of leadership as a one-way street, or is it an ongoing dialogue? If you imagine that the only communication that matters to your employees is what you say to them, then you are missing out on an important element of credibility—leadership as a relationship.[10] Credible leaders understand that communication has to work both ways to be effective.

- **Work as a team.** It is essential to think of yourself as part of a team. When you approach work with a "we" mentality instead of an "I" mentality, you show your employees and stakeholders that you care about them—and about the company—more than you care about yourself.

- **Use Facts and figures.** You can use precision to boost credibility by avoiding generalizations and sticking to specifics. This doesn't mean that you can't express your vision in sweeping terms—but it does mean that you must support broad statements with hard data if you want to appear credible.

- **Honesty.** There will be people who will see straight through a lie and to your hidden agenda. This is an obvious one. If you lie, you lose trust, you lose respect. This is very hard to get back.

- **Start over.** If you mess up, genuinely apologize and ask, "Can we start over?" People will give you a second and even third chance. Ensure that the mistake never happens again and learn from it. Leaders are human, too.

Practical tips for helping you build credibility with a new team

- Early on with a new team, there are a number of critical items to cover that will help you build credibility and trust quickly. These steps are all based on asking your employees for their input and showing interest in their background and motivations—something that many leaders miss.

1. **Your background.** Reaffirm your strengths and the value you bring to the organization as a leader.

2. **Clarify your expectations.** How do you like to work? How do you expect your team to work?

3. **Ask about your team.** What motivates them? What are their strengths, their technical capabilities, background, and experience? What demotivates them?

4. **Set goals.** Ask your team members individually what their goals are in the next 12 months, 3 years, and 5 years—at work and outside of work. This will give you insight into their motivations and how you can help them to achieve their goals. Ask them how you can assist them with achieving their goals. Discuss work goals and objectives and set a plan for the next 6 months to 3 years for the individual.

5. **Performance expectations.** Discuss with each of your subordinates your definition of success and ask them what their definition of success is. Tell them how you will measure their performance. Ask them to what standards they will measure your effectiveness.

6. **The plan moving forward:** Continue to provide and gain feedback from your subordinates. Credibility is something that needs to be maintained.

Key Takeaways

1. Credibility is the foundation of trust and respect.
2. A lack of credibility can damage you individually and professionally.
3. Responding to a crisis in a way that underscores credibility is essential.
4. Leadership is a relationship, not a one-way street.
5. Accepting blame when things go wrong is essential if you want your employees to respect you as a leader.
6. Arguing against your own self-interest is a good way to demonstrate credibility to both employees and clients.
7. You must work for your employees as much as they work for you.
8. Backing up your arguments with precise facts makes it more likely that you will be perceived as credible.

3
Using Psychology to Influence and Persuade

Those who don't know how to get people to say yes soon fall away; those who do, stay and flourish.
~ Robert Cialdini[1]

Effective leaders understand the importance of persuasion. As a leader or business owner, of course it is possible simply to order employees to perform necessary tasks. However, orders do little to inspire loyalty or enthusiasm. Influencing and persuading the people who work for you is much more effective, and as a rule leads to better results, than simply giving orders. Sure, you can use persuasion to manipulate, but the aim here is for the greater good—to help you achieve greater performance through motivated and engaged employees.

The Art of Persuasion

Let's start with a definition of persuasion from a psychological perspective. In <u>The Dynamics of Persuasion,</u> Richard Perloff defines persuasion as:

A symbolic process in which communicators try to convince other people to change their attitudes or behaviors regarding an issue, through the transmission of a message, in an atmosphere of free choice.[2]

To put it simply, persuasion is a way of getting people to do what you want them to do. When you persuade someone, you convince them. If you do it correctly, they should feel that they are doing it because they want to do it—not because you told them to do it. That's an important distinction. People who feel themselves to have been persuaded to do something are more likely to be enthusiastic and thorough than people who feel themselves to have been ordered to do the same thing.

The Psychological Principles of Persuasion

As a leader, what can you do to get people to say yes? There are six psychological principles used by influential leaders to persuade both colleagues and subordinates. They are: reciprocity, commitment, consistency, authority, liking, and scarcity. Each one of these principles is helpful to leaders. Robert Cialdini was the first person to put all of these existing psychological principles together into a theory of persuasion. He spent three years observing influencers in various industries and found that, by and large, they all used the same basic techniques to get what they needed.[3]

Reciprocity

Reciprocity is a phenomenon that exists in many different cultures. On the surface, it bears some resemblance to gift giving. However, it differs from gift giving in that there is no expectation of a return gesture when one gives a gift. Reciprocity carries with it the assumption that, at some point in the future, the favor will be returned.

Just how strong is this human tendency for reciprocity? A 1971 study[4] investigated just this. In the study, participants were told they were in an art appreciation study, and were put in a room with a member of the research team who they were told was another study participant named Joe. During a break, the disguised researcher left the room. Half of the time, he came back with two bottles of Coke, indicating that he had asked the researchers if he could get one for himself and then decided to bring one back for the participant, as well. With the other half of participants, he returned empty-handed.

A little later, "Joe" asked the other person to do him a favor and buy some raffle tickets for $0.25 apiece, telling them that he was in a contest and would win a prize if he sold the most tickets. The study found that the participants who received a Coke from Joe were far more likely to reciprocate by buying raffle tickets than those who received nothing.

The vast majority of us are hardwired in this way, to have a sense of obligation when someone does us a favor.

Commitment and Consistency

Most people place a high premium on the appearance of consistency. When they make a commitment to something, they feel an urge to stick to it even when it goes against their best interest.

For example, a 1975 study looked at the way bystanders on a beach reacted to a staged theft.[5] The control group saw a man placing his things near participants, including a radio which he left out in the open. When he walked away, a "thief" stole the radio. Very few participants chose to intervene, with only four of the 20 subjects making any effort to stop the theft. However, when the first man in the scenario asked nearby people to watch his things, the reactions changed dramatically. 19 of the 20 people asked made a diligent effort to stop the thief, even going so far as to chase him down and grab the radio from him. These people felt a strong obligation to follow through on the commitment they had made despite the fact that attempting to stop a robbery might be dangerous.

In addition, we know that when people commit to something, either verbally or in writing, they are more likely to follow through. For example, in a 1987 study[6], potential voters were approached on the eve of Election Day and asked whether they would vote, and why or why not. 100% said they would vote. Of those who were asked if they would vote, 86.7% went to the polls compared to 61.5% of those who were not asked. Put simply, when we verbally or in writing commit to something we are significantly more likely to follow through.

Authority

People are culturally indoctrinated to respond to and obey authority figures. In certain circumstances, the mere illusion of authority is enough to convince people to behave in a certain way.

A 1963 study at Stanford illustrated the link between authority and persuasion in a dramatic manner.[7] Participants were told they were engaged in a study of memory and were assigned the role of "Teacher." They were placed in a room with a researcher disguised as another participant who was identified as a "Learner." The participants were told that their job was to deliver a series of increasingly intense electrical shocks to the Learner when he got a question from an authority figure (a man in a white coat) wrong.

There were no electrical shocks administered, but the Learners were actors who behaved as if there were. Remarkably, even when the actors begged for mercy, the participants continued to administer shocks at the urging of the authority figure, with two-thirds delivering the maximum shock available. This study clearly indicates the power of authority when it comes to persuasion, as normally the human tendency toward empathy would have prevented such behavior.

Liking

The concept that people are willing to do favors for people they like is hardly surprising. A 1974 study of the Canadian elections showed that attractive candidates, those who the voters found more likeable thanks to something called the Halo Effect, got two and a half times as many votes as unattractive candidates.[8]

Physical attractiveness isn't the only factor when it comes to liking. Similarity plays a role too, just as it did in hiring. A 1971 study showed that students were more likely to grant a favor (handing over a dime for a phone call) to someone who was dressed similarly to them than to someone who wasn't.[9]

Compliments can also play a role, and for the purposes of persuasion, even remembering someone's name can be enough to increase persuasion, as demonstrated by a 1995 study.[10]

The bottom line is that we are easily persuaded into action by people we like.

Scarcity

The final element of persuasion is scarcity. As a rule, people have a tendency to place a higher value on things that are difficult to get than on things that are readily available. While the most obvious example of scarcity is scarcity of numbers (such as when only a limited number of a particular item is available), it can also refer to scarcity of time, as well as to rarity.[11]

How to Use the Principles of Persuasion

Understanding the psychological principles used in the art of persuasion is the first step, but the goal is to make use of them when managing employees. Let's take them one at a time.

1. **Reciprocity** is one of the easiest principles of persuasion to use in the workplace because it is so simple. Giving employees something they perceive to be a gift can go a long way toward building loyalty. For example, a boss who pays for lunch or lets their employees go early before a long weekend reaps a lot of good without actually spending very much. The employees feel gratitude for the boss' generosity, and

are thus willing to go above and beyond as a way of reciprocating.

Reciprocity does not just have to be in the form of money. As a leader, helping an employee with something that they would not expect your help on will encourage reciprocity. Doing an employee a favor, such as being open to holding a meeting later in the day because you know at lunch they like to get out of the office, is a gesture that will encourage feelings of reciprocity.

In using reciprocity, be mindful that the gesture should be genuine and not because of a hidden agenda. Also, be mindful of regular reciprocity delivered in the same form. For example, if you regularly take the same group of people out to lunch, this will become their norm and they will no longer see the action as a gift in which they are inclined to reciprocate. Instead, they will come to expect the gesture.

2. **Commitment and consistency** can be powerful tools when it comes to asking employees to help out with a big project or special assignment. A 1996 study showed that people who said they would be willing to volunteer for a charity overwhelmingly did volunteer when asked to make a commitment after the initial question.[12] An effective leader will use this principle by asking in a meeting which employees would be willing to help with

a particular project and asking them to put their names on a sign-up sheet. The employees will want to avoid appearing inconsistent, and will thus be persuaded to follow through and work on the project.

3. **Authority** is in some ways the most obvious of the principles of persuasion for a leader to use on their subordinates, but it can also be a tricky one. Pulling rank on your employees is necessary at times, but a leader who overdoes it will be seen as a dictator rather than an authority. However, there are some subtle things that will remind employees who is in charge:

   a. **Make sure that your orders are orders and not requests**. If you hand out a task, say, "I require this back to me by noon tomorrow." Not, "Does noonish tomorrow work for you?" When you word it the first way, you remind the employee that you are giving the orders and make it clear that they will have to come to you for an extension if they need more time.

   b. **Have clear boundaries and enforce them**. The rules of the office need to apply to everybody equally, and you must make it clear what they are. If you don't have a written employee handbook or code of conduct, write one and have employees sign and acknowledge it. (Note: this makes use of commitment and consistency, too.)

c. **Be friendly with your employees but keep a line between friendship and work.** Disciplining someone you consider a friend—and who considers you one—is tricky business. The key is to be compassionate without getting involved too much in employees' personal lives.

d. **Don't rule out being stern when needed.** Often persuasion is most effective when it is low-key, but sometimes it is necessary to escalate things. Your desire to use the principles of persuasion should not override your responsibilities. If you must crack down on an employee, do it firmly and decisively.

4. **Being likable** is a very effective way to persuade employees, yet leaders must be very cautious not to blur the lines between work and friendship. An effective and persuasive leader takes the time to learn and use people's names. Franklin D. Roosevelt was renowned for knowing people's names and faces. Learn some personal details about employees, such as the names of their spouses and children. Effective leaders also make a point of asking about hobbies and pastimes. The benefit of learning how employees spend their free time is that it can help to identify similarities, one of

the things that leads to liking. Another thing that can help is to maintain a dress code similar to that of your employees. If you expect employees to wear business attire, so should you. If you tell them to dress casually, you will be more persuasive if you dress in a similar fashion. The goal is to find some forms of common ground.

5. **Use scarcity**. Scarcity is difficult to implement in the workplace. However, if you are gearing up for a big project and will need employees' help, you can tell them that you only have room for five people on your team. The illusion that being on the team is something special can go a long way toward convincing people to sign up to be a part of it.

Used properly, the principles of persuasion can help you to make your employees into enthusiastic and willing members of your team.

Key Takeaways

1. Cialdini's Principles of Persuasion are basic techniques that are used by leaders in every field.
2. Reciprocity is an effective way to create a sense of obligation in your employees.

3. Commitment and consistency allow you to use persuasion to get your employees to commit to doing something and then reap the benefits of their need to be seen as consistent.

4. Using authority to influence employees requires drawing clear boundaries and enforcing them without coming across as a dictator.

5. Liking allows you to use things such as wardrobe and similarities with your employees to generate cooperation.

6. Scarcity is a way of enticing employees to do something they might not otherwise want to do by making it seem like an exclusive opportunity.

4
The Psychology of Modesty and Humility in Leaders

Humility is the true key to success. Successful people lose their way at times. They often embrace and overindulge from the fruits of success. Humility halts this arrogance and self-indulging trap. Humble people share the credit and wealth, remaining focused and hungry to continue the journey of success.

~ Rick Pitino

It might seem paradoxical for leaders to establish authority over subordinates while also demonstrating modesty and humility. However, the two characteristics go hand in hand. A leader who can be modest about their own achievements and rank is one who can inspire great loyalty from employees. Understanding the psychology of modesty can help a good leader become a great one.

Identifying Modesty and Humility

In <u>Modesty, Humility, Character Strength, and Positive Psychology</u>, Harvey and Pauwels define modesty as:

Not regarding oneself as more special than one is.[1]

In other words, a person who is modest is one who is not arrogant—who sees themselves clearly and does not self-aggrandize.

The Paradox of Modesty

It is important to acknowledge that there is, inherent in the idea of being modest about one's accomplishments or rank, a paradox. Traditionally, the philosophy of virtue has argued that to be kind, one must be aware that one is being kind, and so on. However, to say, "I am modest," feels like an immodest act.[2]

It is possible to resolve this paradox simply by realizing that modesty is not about a lack of self-awareness. Rather, modesty is about a high degree of self-awareness, as well as an awareness of the effect that talking at length about one's own accomplishments will have on other people.[3] It is helpful to think of modesty as a conscious behavior rather than an innate quality.

Awareness of Modesty

By the age of eight, children are found to exhibit a preference for modest statements of accomplishments over immodest ones.[4] Studies have also found a direct correlation between children's abilities to read social situations properly and their preferences for modest statements. In other words, a tendency toward modesty actually increased their social aptitude and even their social standing.

Interestingly, there appears to be a cultural divide on the topic of modesty. Western cultures, particularly in the United States, tend to have what is known as the Self-Serving Bias.[5] This means that, as a rule, people who live in western cultures tend to give themselves credit for positive outcomes, and others the blame for negative ones. That tendency is reversed in Japan and some other Asian countries.[6] People there exhibit the opposite of a Self-Serving Bias, something known as the Modesty Bias. The Japanese people, as a rule, tend to blame themselves when things go wrong, and pass the praise to others when they go right.

When it comes to modesty, leaders in the West can face an uphill battle. They have to overcome their tendency toward the Self-Serving Bias and use modesty as a leadership trait.

Humility and Social Bonds

One interesting benefit of humble leadership is that it confirms something called the Social Bonds Hypothesis. This theory says that the human ability to form cooperative relationships, such as those required in a healthy work environment, is contingent upon a mechanism being in place to help avoid exploitation.[7] When subordinates view their leaders as humble, they are far more likely to cooperate with them than they would be if their leaders appeared to be egotistical or self-serving.

Humility and Competition

Encouraging a high level of performance and healthy competition is important in any successful workplace. However, competition can make friendly relations among leaders and subordinates difficult. Humility can be the solution, due to a psychological effect known as the Social Oil Hypothesis.[8] The Social Oil Hypothesis says that humility optimizes the benefits of competition by buffering the impact that competition can have on social relationships. Similar to the manner in which oil prevents an engine from overheating, humility reduces the damage of competitive traits such as high standards or competitiveness.

Humility has a way of smoothing out the competitive edges and making the notion of competition more palatable than it would be if one or more of the parties involved were egotistical. Demonstrating humble leadership can make a huge difference in the overall social atmosphere of a company.

Examples of Humble Leadership

In order to get a better idea of the benefits of humble leadership, let's look at several real-life examples.

Pixar Studios

The first example comes from the movie studio Pixar. For a long time, when Pixar held meetings to discuss their work, the meetings took place in a large conference room with a rectangular table.[9] At first the seating arrangements were informal, but the director of the film being discussed and the management team at Pixar needed to be heard by everybody, so they occupied seats at the center of the table. Over time, it became commonplace to make place cards for the meetings.

Ed Catmull, the head of Pixar, noticed that the people who were seated at the ends of the table—those lower down in the Pixar hierarchy—were not contributing to the conversation. What's interesting is that he didn't notice this until the company was forced to hold a meeting in a smaller room with a square table. Suddenly, everyone in the meeting was contributing to the conversation. Their input was valuable and necessary, and the management team realized it.

How did they deal with it? They took the big, rectangular table out of their usual conference room, banished the place cards, and welcomed everyone into the conversation. This resulted in meetings that were more lively and productive than previous meetings had been, and which served the company better.

The takeaway here is that, at least sometimes, apparent hierarchy is not a good thing. The new set-up of the table represented the leaders' humility in not needing to be "at the head of the table," so to speak.

Warren Buffett

Warren Buffett is one of the world's most visible businessmen. His net worth is estimated at $47 billion, and he is often asked for economic and financial advice. It would perhaps be understandable if a man who has achieved so much were arrogant, yet Buffett lives (and leads) in surprisingly humble ways.

One example of Buffett's humble leadership style is that he draws a salary of only $100,000 from his company, Berkshire Hathaway.[10] In 2015, he even sent a warning to his eventual successor that said, "Don't be greedy." Many CEOs draw huge salaries, and that can increase their susceptibility to the Self-Serving Bias. That's not to suggest that every leader must cut their salary in order to be modest, but there is something to be learned from Buffett's attitude. He still lives in the same house in Omaha he bought more than 50 years ago, and his humble nature carries over into his leadership style. Buffet's humble leadership style included explaining what he is doing, in simple language, so that everyone understands. He admits mistakes and does not try to sugar-coat them, like when he admitted "serious errors I made in my job of capital allocation...". He then said "I will commit more errors; you can count on that." These are some of the traits that make Buffet's leadership style stand out.

Richard Branson

Richard Branson is a hugely successful entrepreneur who is famous for his humble leadership style. He credits his success at Virgin with two traits that typify modesty in leadership— listening and learning.[11] A person who is lacking in humility is likely to be neither a good listener, nor willing to admit they have something to learn. In contrast, Richard Branson demonstrates humility by valuing, listening, and learning from other people in his company.

The Price of a Lack of Humility

Before looking at some ways that leaders can bring humility to the workplace, let's look at an example of what can happen in the absence of humility. A 2009 study found that a significant percentage of operating-room errors happened because surgeons did not create an environment where nurses felt that they could voice their concerns in the middle of surgery.[12] Hierarchy was made very apparent and nursing roles were seen largely as serving the purpose of creating a calming environment for the surgeons. The issue with this however, was that the nurses often picked up errors, errors that meant the difference between life and death to the patients in their care. What we know now is that breaking down barriers created by hierarchy—such as not knowing how, or feeling that it is not okay, to speak out against an authority—can improve results for patients in hospital settings, by improving communication among hospital workers.

Practical Ways to Bring Humility to the Workplace

There are three key factors to humble leadership: always being willing to admit mistakes, acknowledging that there are still things you can learn, and sharing credit for successes. Let's talk about each one.

Admitting Mistakes

The first thing you can do to demonstrate humble leadership—to be the oil that the Social Oil Hypothesis calls for—is to be willing to admit when you make a mistake. Nobody likes to admit that they've done something wrong, but the ability to do so is a hallmark of true leadership.

Remember that the qualities of the Self-Serving Bias include a tendency to take credit when the results are good, and assign blame when the results are bad. An effective leader needs to do the opposite. One famous example of a leader willing to take the blame was President Harry S. Truman. He kept a sign that said "The Buck Stops Here" on his desk as a reminder to himself and others that leadership involves taking responsibility when things don't go as planned.

When something goes wrong in your department or company, the key thing to remember is that, ultimately, everything that happens there is under your leadership. When an employee makes a mistake or drops the ball, the fact is that you are responsible for supervising that employee. A leader who steps up and accepts the blame is one who employees will respect. It might not be easy to shoulder the responsibility for a mistake, but the willingness to do so is one of the essential hallmarks of leadership.

Modeling Teachability

The second key characteristic of humble leaders is a willingness to do two important things:

1. To admit when they don't know something; and
2. To be willing to learn on an ongoing basis.

A leader who is affected by the Self-Serving Bias always seeks to place blame on other people. It is also very common for leaders to feel that they need to know everything, and that their vast knowledge has earned them the big seat. These attitudes, however, result in difficulty admitting a lack of knowledge about any topic. The problems in this are that you don't grow as a person and you demonstrate to your employees that you think you know it all. That's a dangerous attitude to have, especially in a situation where it has just been demonstrated that you don't know it all. Instead, you should model to your employees that nobody knows everything. This is why different people from different departments are employed—to contribute their varied expertise.

The desire to learn goes hand in hand with the ability to shoulder the blame. They both show a willingness to accept your own vulnerabilities and shortcomings in a way that shows employees that it is also safe for them to do so. When leaders demonstrate this type of modesty, they make it easy for employees to admit to mistakes, as well—and to ask for help. Would you rather have an employee who covers up mistakes and refuses to learn, or one who readily admits to mistakes and is eager to add to their knowledge base? The answer is obvious, and the only way to get the second kind of employee is to show your subordinates what you expect by modeling it on a daily basis.

Sharing Credit

The third and final hallmark of modest leadership is a tendency to share the credit with subordinates in the wake of a big success. Contrasting the Self-Serving Bias and the Social

Oil Hypothesis is important. The Self-Serving Bias gives us the tendency to look for someone to blame after a failure and makes us reluctant to share credit after a win. At the same time, the Social Oil Hypothesis tells us that humility reduces the damage of competitive traits such as high standards or competitiveness

A modest leader is always willing to share the credit with their employees. Why? Because they know that they never act alone. Any leader—in any field of endeavor—relies on the support and skills of their subordinates. No General goes into battle alone, just as no leader approaches a big project alone. If you try to grab all the credit for yourself, your employees will (rightfully) resent you. As a result, they will be less willing to help you in the future.

The next time you experience a big success, do whatever you can to share the credit with your team. Sharing credit does not need to include financial compensation—although, at times, that is certainly appropriate. A congratulatory speech or email, or a small expenditure like a celebratory drink, can be enough to let your employees know that you understand and appreciate the contributions they have made.

A leader who can willingly shoulder the blame for their own mistakes and the mistakes of their team, demonstrate a willingness to learn, and regularly share the credit for their successes, is a leader who can inspire great loyalty and enthusiasm. While there are times when a show of authority is necessary, modesty and humility go a great way toward earning the respect and admiration of your team.

Key Takeaways

1. Awareness of modesty seems at first glance to be paradoxical, but true modesty requires the ability to take the feelings of others into consideration.

2. The Self-Serving Bias is typified by a desire to cast around for someone to blame when things go wrong, and to grab the credit when things go well.

3. The Modesty Bias is the opposite, and is more common in Eastern culture than in Western culture.

4. The Social Bonds Hypothesis and the Social Oil Hypothesis demonstrate the necessity for humility in leadership when it comes to encouraging a good social environment and healthy bonds in the workplace.

5. A willingness to admit mistakes and shoulder the blame for department- or company-wide failures is the first hallmark of a great leader. Remember that "The buck stops here" and apply it to your own work.

6. The ability to confess when you don't know something, coupled with a willingness to constantly learn, is the second hallmark of a great leader. When you model

teachability for your employees, you greatly increase the likelihood that they will be willing to admit their own mistakes, ask for help when needed, and learn new things that will make them better employees.

7. The willingness to share credit in the wake of a big success is the third hallmark of humble leadership. Even small gestures of acknowledgement, such as a thank you email or speech, can go a long way toward demonstrating your humility to your subordinates.

5
The Psychology of Power

Nearly all men can stand adversity, but if you want to test a man's character, give him power.
~ often attributed to Abraham Lincoln

Power in leaders is often misunderstood. People tend to view power as a form of absolutism—as a way of controlling others, with an iron fist if necessary. However, there is more than one way to define power, and certainly more than one way to use it.

What Is Power?

The traditional definition of power refers to the influence a leader has over a group of people.

The most effective form of a leader's power, however, is power *through* a group rather than over them.[1] An effective leader does not flaunt their power over others by coercing subordinates to do what is necessary. Instead, they find ways to convert them to new ways of thinking.

The psychological definition of power says that when power exists, the relationship between person A and person B is such that when A attempts to influence B, a change in B is more likely than it would be in the absence of power.[2]

This can be broken down further into five types of power[3] leaders have:

1. **Coercive power** is power that relies upon the threat of negative consequences, such as demotion or firing, in order to compel action. This form of power has limited effectiveness and will even undermine a leader's goals if it is used too frequently.

2. **Reward power** is power that uses the promise of incentives such as praise, promotions, or raises, in order to achieve a goal. This form of power can be effective, but can also have a significant impact if withdrawn.

3. **Legitimate power** is power conveyed by virtue of a leader's position relative to subordinates. For example, a CEO or president has legitimate power, but will lose it if they lose their title.

4. **Expert power** is power linked to a leader's knowledge or experience. A person who has a great deal of specialized information will naturally fall into a leadership role as a result of their knowledge.

5. **Referent power** is the result of subordinates liking and respecting a leader. Because referent power has more to do with personality than competence, it can be easily abused.

All five kinds of power have their place. However, the effective use of each kind of power depends on the situation, time, place and audience. Even a valuable kind of power like referent power can be misused.

The Dark Side of Leadership

Power can be used for good—as when it helps leaders motivate employees and make important changes. However, it can also be a corrosive and harmful force.

Subordinates are most likely to perceive abuse of power and feel powerless when leaders withhold information, work toward a hidden agenda, or lack transparency.

One study in the *Journal of Personality and Social Psychology* examined the psychological link between self-interest and power. It found that certain leaders who had a high level of self-interest were more likely to put their own needs and desires ahead of those of the group. This was true even if it meant that the group failed to achieve their goals.[4] In one case, group leaders were given information crucial to the success of the task. Confident leaders who knew how to use power effectively shared the information with the group. Leaders who lacked confidence withheld it.

In the same study, a group of managers were told that one person in their group had extensive, specialized knowledge that would help the group succeed in their appointed task. The effective managers made a point of using their experts to great effect, ensuring that their skill and knowledge were put to use to help the group. The ineffective managers did the opposite—they minimized the expert's participation because they perceived it as a threat to their power.

The paradox of power is that the very traits that enable a person to rise to a position of power are often the traits that disappear once in that position of power. Of course, sometimes these traits that disappear can give way to valuable, new traits—but sometimes not. Common changes include leaders becoming less empathetic to employee concerns, becoming more reliant on stereotypes and generalizations, and showing increases in hypocrisy where the sense of power makes it easier to rationalize away ethical lapses in oneself but not others.

Consistently, research demonstrates that a primary use of coercive leadership results in leaders being rated as less effective. Leaders who fail to clearly define the organizational goals and fail to communicate their expectations are also found to be significantly less effective leaders than leaders who do.[5] In all of these cases, the lesson is clear. In order to be effective, power must be generous and open. When a leader withholds information for selfish reasons, the performance of the group as a whole suffers. If, on the other hand, the leader displays a confident use of appropriate power in a given situation, the group's performance improves and individual members of the group feel empowered and valued. A thoughtful and responsible use of power can be transformative.

Why People Seek Power

The desire for power is a basic human characteristic. In fact, research shows that people seek power so that they can do what they want in life.[6] There is the perception that powerful people can act like themselves rather than having to act in a way that others expect.

People also report a greater sense of satisfaction when they feel in control and that they can act more authentically. A study by psychologist David C. McClelland revealed that leaders rated themselves as happier when they felt that they were in control.[7]

It is important to note, however, that while studies have shown having power can make you happier, studies also show that *seeking* power does not make you happier.

The Price of Power

While the desire for power is a basic human characteristic, it is also extremely common for leaders to fail to take into account the costs of power. The benefits of power—influence and respect—can be great, but the costs of power can include:

1. **Intense publicity and scrutiny**. People who are in power are held to a higher standard than the general population. Consider the case of former Boeing CEO Harry Stonecipher, who had a consensual affair with a Boeing vice president. Although there was no indication of any impropriety or sexual harassment, the board still requested—and received—his resignation.[8] Such scrutiny might not seem fair, but it is commonplace. Psychologically speaking, we tend to be less forgiving of mistakes when they are made by people who have power.

2. **Trading power for autonomy**. People who are in a position of power have more demands on their time and energy, and they often end up missing out on the chance to control their own schedules.

3. **Giving up time and effort**. Many people who are in positions of power find that they simply do not have the time to do things they previously thought were important, including spending time with loved ones. It

can be difficult to sustain close relationships when your job takes so much from you.

4. **Difficulty in trusting others**. One study revealed that nearly 85% of Americans think that they could do the job of their boss at least as well as—if not better than—the person who currently held the job.[9] Ross Johnson, the former CEO of Nabisco, gained a certain amount of notoriety by repeatedly gaining the trust of—and then taking the jobs of—CEOs with whom he worked.[10]

It is important for anybody who seeks power to acknowledge that it comes with a price, and to find ways to maintain balance without sacrificing leadership in the process.

How and Why People Lose Power

One pattern that repeats itself consistently throughout history is that people who have power lose it. Sometimes the loss of power is an orderly transition, such as an election. Other times, loss of power takes the form of a coup or a fall from grace. Here, we are concerned with the last two. How do people who have power lose it? What mistakes do they make, and how can you use psychological principles to avoid them?

1. **Overconfidence**. The first thing that can lead to a loss of power is overconfidence. In 2011 Shipman identified that leaders who are overconfident can over expect

positive outcomes and be less aware of their deficits. The study found that visions and plans are negatively impacted by overconfidence in leaders. Overconfident leaders were less likely to identify deficiencies/problems/obstacle in idea development phase.[11] While studies have shown that confidence is beneficial to leadership success, overconfidence is not.

2. **Misplaced trust, or too much trust**. The more isolated you are from reality, the easier it can be to take someone else's word for the way things are. One classic example is former Bank of America CEO David Coulter, who lost his job after believing the reassurances he received from Nations Bank during the 1998 merger of the two companies.[12] The lesson here is being too trusting or not vigilant can result in leaders losing power.

3. **Lack of patience**. Being a leader often requires you to suppress your personal feelings about people and situations in order to get things done. It is also common to be bombarded with opinions about what you're doing and how you're doing it—something related to scrutiny—and it can be difficult to maintain your patience and motivation when you are constantly being scrutinized. Either way, I have seen on a number of occasions where lack of patience has eroded a leader's power.

4. **Lack of adaptability.** Being flexible is a crucial skill in the business world. Being inflexible, in contrast, can sink leaders—and companies. Often, we get caught up in doing things in a particular way. Because our old methods worked well in the past, we continue to use them, and fail to see when things change around us, or in the world at large. A leader who lacks the ability to adapt to changing circumstances is unlikely to retain power for long. A few companies that immediately come to mind that failed to adapt include Blockbuster, Kodak (noted in chapter 1) and Blackberry.

5. **Trying to control everything.** Sharing power and leadership are predictors of organizational success or failure. Leaders who hold on to power the most tightly—and refuse to share it—are far more likely to lose it than those who adopt a more generous leadership style.[13] Furthermore, employees who feel that they are part of a decision-making process are more likely to do what leaders want them to do.[14] So, encourage participative decision making where possible.

6. **Competing against other leaders.** When leaders compete with one another using displays of power, the organization suffers as a result. Instead, leaders who work toward the greater good, who are less focused on hierarchy, and who are less focused on *appearing* to

be better than others, are more likely to succeed longer term than those who insist on inappropriate power displays.[15] Collaborating and maintaining positive relationships with your fellow leaders also enables you to turn to them for help during times of crisis—an important resilience resource for you.

7. **Making inconsistent decisions.** Leaders will struggle to build trust and maintain power when decisions, or follow through of decisions, are not consistent, fair, and communicated well.[16] Leaders who do a good job of explaining their rationale to employees, are consistent and fair in their decision making, and follow through on commitments, are more likely to maintain referent power than leaders who do not.

8. **Burn out.** When you do a job for a long time, you will sometimes end up feeling exhausted or burnt out. When this happens, you are not at your best. For a leader, this can open the door for someone else to come in and take power away.

Nobody holds on to power forever, but it is certainly possible to avoid some of the things that can erode or even destroy power. It is important to remember that, even in non-democratic situations such as private companies, leaders derive their power from their subordinates. In other words, leadership is not monolithic. To be effective, power must be built upon a sturdy base—and that base is your employees.[17]

Lessons for Leaders

Let's look at some practical tools that will help you maintain your power as a leader. Each of these lessons can be applied to any leadership situation, whether you manage a small department or lead a huge multinational corporation.

- **Empower and delegate.** There will be situations where you will need to take control. However, there will also be times where you do not need to be in primary control. For example, is there a meeting that you can let someone else lead, or a project that someone else has the capability and drive to lead? Micromanagement is rarely successful. Instead of clinging to power, try sharing it with your employees.

  Delegate decisions when you can and empower people to make certain decisions on their own, and then sit back to observe people flourishing. Of course, such empowerment must be earned, and then supervised—but, in general, employees will perform at a high level when they feel that you trust them.

- **Invite participative decision making.** The majority of decisions in organizations will inevitably come from the top down. However, rather than handing down decisions unilaterally—a use of coercive power—find areas where you can adopt a participatory decision-making process. This approach initiates change from the bottom up. To do this, it is important to be clear with staff where you will seek their input so that they do not come to expect that they will be involved in all decisions. Boundaries are still needed and leaders still have the prerogative to make final decisions.

One strategy that can help is giving people options. You can define three options and then give people a choice between these options. You decide the options and asking people to select an option, rather than handing over all the power of choice. When employees believe that they play some role in decision making, they will show greater commitment, motivation, and loyalty.

When asking for input, also genuinely show that you value other people's opinions and that you are open to different opinions. It is not your role to be an expert at everything. This is why you employ people.

- **Share the 'why'**. When you instruct your employees to do something, also provide them with an explanation or rationale as to why this task/goal is important. Sell them the 'why' first before the 'what' and the 'how'. Unilateral demands are far more likely to be perceived as irrational or unfair than requests that are accompanied by an explanation for why they are important. Translate for staff "What's in it for me?"

- **Servant leadership**. Remember that your employees are the source of your power, and treat them accordingly. You are the leader, but if your employees won't do what you need them to do, your power will be eroded as a result. Look at that as a positive thing, and embrace what your employees have to offer. Do what you can to increase opportunities for other people instead of diminishing them. No employee likes to feel underutilized. Let your employees shine, and it will reflect well on you, too.

As you can see, the one thing that is true in every situation is that holding on tightly to power is a good way to lose it. The more open and generous you are with the power you have attained, the more likely you are to be able to make changes and influence your organization in a positive way.

Key Takeaways

1. Power is not having power over people, but rather finding avenues to power through people by converting subordinates to new ways of thinking.

2. The five kinds of power are coercive power, reward power, legitimate power, expert power, and referent power.

3. The desire for power is a fundamental human drive—not the desire to control people, but rather the desire to influence them. Power is important because it drives everything that happens in an organization, including major decisions and changes.

4. Power is not a bad thing in and of itself. However, it can turn into something dangerous when leaders withhold necessary information, or when they refuse to use employees' strengths out of fear.

5. Nobody achieves a position of power without paying a price. Some of the things leaders must face when they attain power include increased scrutiny of their actions, a decrease in autonomy, a diminution of their free time, a need to sacrifice things that were once thought important, and their ability to trust the people around them.

6. Some of the reasons that people lose power include overconfidence, misplaced trust, impatience, burnout/exhaustion, and a lack of adaptability.

7. The lessons you can learn about power are:

    a. Don't be afraid to delegate authority and empower your employees

b. Solicit opinions and suggestions from employees when making major decisions

c. Collaborate and share information with other leaders during times of crisis

d. Instead of handing down unilateral commands, explain your rationale for doing things a certain way

e. Remember that you derive your power from your employees; treat them accordingly

f. Find ways to maximize the possibilities for your employees instead of diminishing them

8. Remember that, on the whole, those leaders who hold on to power the longest are those who are the most generous with what they have and what they know. Power is not a weapon. When used properly, it is a force for positive change.

6
Using Psychology to Build Resilience

The moment we believe that success is determined by an ingrained level of ability as opposed to resilience and hard work, we will be brittle in the face of adversity.
~ Joshua Waitzkin

Every leader, no matter how great, suffers an occasional setback or defeat. What sets great leaders apart from the more mediocre is the way they rebound from loss. A good leader is a resilient leader, and the reason for that is clear. Nobody wants to follow a person who's not resilient. If a small defeat turns into a bad attitude and an unwillingness to press, employees will stop taking their leader seriously.

What Is Psychological Resilience?

If you have ever seen a stretched rubber band snap back, you have seen resilience in action. The capacity of the band to stretch without breaking demonstrates its ability to endure outside forces. Psychological resilience is similar. A simple definition of psychological resilience is:

The ability of an individual to adapt to stress and adversity, and to thrive in spite of the presence of those things.[1]

Some of the key characteristics demonstrated by people with a high degree of psychological resilience include:[2]

- Facing reality (not glossing over the facts)
- Ritualized ingenuity (seeking out solutions to problems)
- The ability to exploit the positive events in life
- Proactive problem solving
- Recognition of the need to change
- A tendency to face problems head-on rather than avoiding them
- Early recognition of a need to change
- The ability to keep things in perspective
- The ability to look for meaning in life
- Knowing where to look for assistance when necessary

The Nicholson McBride Resiliency Questionnaire covers 23 traits that distinguish between people who are, and are not, psychologically resilient.[3] Researchers using the questionnaire found that the most resilient people are those who are optimistic, free from stress and anxiety, accountable for their own actions, open and flexible, and oriented toward problem solving.[4]

Starting in the 1970s, researchers Emmy Warner and Ruth Smith studied the resilience of 505 children born in Kauai, many of whom had alcoholic or abusive parents.[5] They wanted to see how those children adapted to the adversity in which they grew up. They found that, as the children grew, roughly two-thirds of them demonstrated adverse effects from their upbringing, including substance abuse and chronic unemployment. However, one-third of the subjects were able to thrive despite the adversity they had faced. Those children were the ones who had the highest levels of psychological resilience.

How to Develop Resilience as a Leader

We all have the ability to develop resilience. Some of us may not have been raised in an environment that encouraged resilience, but that doesn't mean that we lack the ability to become more resilient. This section will explore some concrete things you can do to develop resilience as a leader.

One thing to keep in mind is that, while resilience is important for both leaders and subordinates, it is not something you can force upon your employees. There is no matrix you can give them to use that will make them become more resilient. The most you can hope for is to develop resilience as a leader and model that behavior for your employees. Do not underestimate the power of such modeling. Imagine how demoralized the rank and file soldiers in an army would be if their general saw an attacking force and said, "We're doomed." How hard would they fight? When you demonstrate an unwillingness to be beaten down by circumstances, your employees are far more likely to model your behavior than to contradict it.

Perspective

The first thing you must do to cultivate resilience is to become skilled at putting setbacks into perspective. People who have a very negative mindset often have a hard time doing this when they run into a setback or disappointment. They have a fixed mindset that tells them that they have failed and that there is no way out of the situation.

The key to becoming someone who can put things into perspective quickly is to cultivate a growth mindset.[6] A growth mindset tells you that anything that happens to you is an opportunity to learn and grow. People who approach adversity with this point of view tend to rebound much more quickly because they are able, even in the midst of a difficult situation, to understand that long-term benefits come from learning to cope with it. You can cultivate a growth mindset by doing the following:

- Seeking out opportunities to learn new things

- Seeking out (and accepting) constructive criticism
- Forming a realistic view of your own characteristics and abilities
- Letting go of past resentments and disappointments by reframing them—this requires looking at what you learned as a result of these negative events

A leader who can do the above things will have a very healthy perspective on life and work.

Refusing to be a Victim of Circumstances

When bad things happen to you, do you take them personally or do you realize that everybody has to encounter some adversity in life? The people who tend to take setbacks personally also tend to be the least able to bounce back from disappointments or losses. If you view yourself as a victim, you are going to behave like a victim—and that's not what you want to model for your employees.

One common cause for such a mindset is the tendency to get caught up in your personal history instead of looking at possibilities.[7] If you tend to look backward instead of forward, you will need to find a way to let go of what has happened to you in the past and believe that you can find a new way to do things going forward.

Some of the things you can do to stop thinking like a victim include:

- Stop placing blame on others when things go wrong
- Practice gratitude for the good things around you
- Let go of past resentments (as you can see, this is related to perspective, too)
- Act confident to be confident

No matter how pushed down you feel by a setback, it's important to show your subordinates that you are confident and capable. If you act like a victim of circumstances, they are going to feel that the same is true of them—and of your department or company. If, on the other hand, you demonstrate an ability to shoulder responsibility and be proactive, they will be more confident in their own ability to deal with adversity.

Focusing on What You Can Control

As mentioned previously, one of the key characteristics of people who are psychologically resilient is self-efficacy—the belief in one's ability to succeed in specific situations.[8] People with high self-efficacy believe they have the ability to control certain things, such as their thoughts and actions, and they put their energy into doing exactly that.

It is important to note here that trying to control everything when something goes wrong is a mistake. Not only is that impossible, but it's also a waste of your valuable time and energy. Being able to identify those things that you cannot control is just as important as knowing what you can control. For example, you can neither control the thoughts and actions of other people, nor can you travel back in time and change the past.

One way to cultivate this aspect of psychological resilience is to practice identifying those things you *can* control. While those things vary from situation to situation, a good rule of thumb is to start with yourself. You can control what you do, and what you say. You can control how you react. In rare circumstances, you can control other things by instructing employees to behave in a particular way or doing particular things. However, even when you give an order, you don't have full control over the outcome. Once you realize that, you can put your focus on the things that you can control.

Accepting Help when Needed

The final thing you can do to help develop resilience is to learn how and when to accept help from other people. As a leader, you may feel that you always have to go it alone. However, that view is not a particularly healthy one and can lead to problems.

Teamwork is an essential component of resilience.[9] When people band together and work toward a common cause, they tend to support one another in the same way that a series of beams support a roof. Groups of people bolster each other—for people this means bolstering confidence and offering different perspectives.

To learn to accept help, work on building a network of people whom you can rely upon in difficult circumstances. Make sure to choose wisely. You will need someone to confide in when you feel a lack of confidence, but that confidante should not be a subordinate—or even someone who works at your company. Instead, turn to a trusted friend or relative. When it comes to seeking help with work problems, remember that letting employees know that you are all part of the same team is a good way to get help.

Case Study – Alan Mulally and the Ford Motor Company

In 2006, Alan Mulally took over as CEO of Ford Motor Company. At the time, the company was at an all-time low. Most outside observers thought that bankruptcy was inevitable. While Mulally was not at the helm during Ford's decline, there is a lot to be learned from the way he approached bringing the company back from the brink of annihilation.[10]

Here are some of the things that Mulally did that demonstrate his own resilience and how he used it to revive Ford:

1. He eliminated turf battles and infighting by creating "One Team" and letting everybody know that they were working for "One Ford."

2. He partnered with the United Auto Workers to make changes that would boost Ford's profitability and bring production jobs back to the United States.

3. He personally pitched Ford's case to banks. By admitting what had gone wrong and being honest about what the company needed to do to rebound, he rebuilt their credibility and got the money he needed.

4. He was confident enough in Ford's ability to survive that he refused money from the federal government after the economic downturn in 2008, but he went to Washington to testify on behalf of his fellow auto companies.

In these four examples, Mulally demonstrated many of the key characteristics we have discussed, including:

- Teamwork
- Asking for help when needed
- Self-confidence
- Accepting control for the things he could control

- The ability to put things into perspective
- Being proactive

Lessons for Leaders

Below are some additional practical tools that you can use to put into practice the key psychological principles of resilience. These tools will help you inside and outside of work, and can be taught to others in your organization.

1. **Sleep.** Sleep clears your brain of toxins, and a lack of sleep is strongly linked to death rates. People who experience a lack of sleep also tend to eat more and experience higher levels of cortisol, which also increases stress levels.

    The importance of sleep is well documented and in a recent study where rats were deprived of sleep indefinitely, results revealed that, within 17 to 21, days their immune systems completely broke down. Despite eating more to help refuel their energy, they all died.[11]

2. **Breaks.** Just because you see employees busy or working longer hours does not mean that they are getting more work done. People who take intermittent breaks to renew their energy tend to be more productive and focused at work.

A study on medical interns revealed that interns who worked the traditional 30 hour shifts made 36% more serious medical errors than interns who worked a staggered schedule, got more breaks, and worked no longer than 16 hours at a time. Errors included ordering drug overdoses, missing a diagnosis of Lyme disease, administering drugs known to provoke an allergy, and trying to drain fluid from the wrong lung. Interns who worked longer shifts without a break were also 5 times more likely to stab themselves and twice as likely to have a car crash on the way home.[12]

It can take as little as a 60 second break to experience recovery.

3. **Mindfulness.** The mind processes 126 pieces of information every second. Mindfulness helps you become more aware of your thoughts and feelings so that instead of being overwhelmed, you are better able to manage. Mindfulness is different from relaxation. Being in a relaxed state can help you to be more mindful but mindfulness is all about focusing your attention. Three ways that you can hone your mindfulness are:

   a. **Mindfulness breathing.** Breathing exercises are effective because your breath is something that you can always access no matter where you are. Breathing works by calming your nervous system and controlling your body's involuntary functions including reducing your heart rate and lactic acid build up. Breathing helps you to calm your mind and can be a great way to start the day.

Find a quiet space and focus on only your breathing, nothing else. If you find that your mind wanders that is okay. Just go back to focusing on your breadth. With practice you can start to pay attention to how you are feeling in the present moment. You can think about how your body is feeling and what your energy levels are like. When you first start, a good target is to aim for 5 minutes of meditative breathing. Gradually, and with practice, you can increase to 20 minutes.

b. **Reflection.** Reflecting on situations can help you to open up your perspective and think about alternative possibilities, including what may change when you make different choices.

Write your thoughts down in a diary on a regular basis. For most people 10 to 15 minutes, 3 or 4 times per week, is effective. You can use a computer, book, or voice recording app. When writing down your thoughts it is important that you do not do other tasks, such as watching TV, at the same time. Your priority for that 15 minutes is to focus only on your reflection. Reflect on how a situation might change if you took an alternative approach. Think about the positives and negatives.

4. **Stress breathing**. When you feel stressed, your breathing rate and pattern changes. This prompts a stress response in your body. Fortunately, you can deliberately change your breathing to help you relax, think clearly, and manage stress responses. To do this, make your body comfortable, whether you are standing or sitting. Breathe in for a count of 3 seconds, hold for 2 seconds, and then breathe out for 4 seconds. Repeat and just focus on your breath. After the third time, you should start to feel your body relax. You can do this in a meeting without anyone knowing.

5. **Positive thinking and being open to possibilities.** For years no one believed that the 100m sprint could be run in less than 10 seconds. Some came close. And then some came closer. And then some came closer still. And the closer runners got to the 10-second, 100-meter sprint, the more people talked negatively about how it couldn't be done. That is until Jim Hines went and did it.

Interestingly, once the 10-second barrier was broken, a flurry of athletes soon managed the same feat. After Hines, everyone knew that it was possible, and so the physical and psychological barrier of the 100-meter, 10-second sprint became less significant.

This example shows the power of positive thinking and belief that something could be possible. There are many other great benefits to positive thinking including:

a. Positive people live longer.

b. Organizations with positive work cultures tend to outperform organizations with negative work cultures.

c. Optimistic salespeople sell more than pessimistic sales people.

d. Positive leaders make better-informed decisions.

e. Positive thinking helps to broaden awareness of the bigger picture.

f. Positive people see more possibilities in life which in turn helps them to be more positive.

The idea around positive thinking and positive psychology is a very simple one. While it's not meant to be complex, difficulty comes with putting it into practice.

a. Tool—Consider at least one alternative and realistic explanation for every negative situation that you face.

b. Tool—Look for solutions, not problems. Focusing on problems stifles your abilities to find innovative solutions and be forward thinking. People who are focused on problems tend to react more negatively than those who are focused on solutions.

6. **Setting mini goals.** When you are stressed, your frontal lobes—responsible for logical thinking–become narrower in their focus. Setting mini goals can direct your focus and trick your brain into thinking that the big task ahead is achievable (which it is). When there is a difficult challenge ahead, focus on what is important and on the small steps you can take to get you to your desired goal.

7. **Finding meaning.** Ask yourself, 'Why is this important?' If you know why something is important then overcoming roadblocks becomes easier. What we know from neuroscience is that people will persevere much longer if something is important to them.[13]

For example, can you run a marathon?

If you said yes, then can you run 2 back to back marathons?

Now, think of the one person that means the most to you. Stop reading this book and spend one minute thinking about this person and how much they mean to you.

Now, imagine that this person is going to die. Today. The only way you can save them is if you run two back to back marathons without stopping. You are the only person who can do it. You will need to run one marathon, get the life-saving vial of medicine, and then run back the second marathon. You cannot stop because if you do then you will see them die in front of you.

Can you run the marathon now?

Find the meaning because this will help you to endure much more stress. Motivation drives purpose.

Resilience is something we all have the ability to cultivate and learn. Past disappointments and challenges make it difficult for us to do so, but part of being a leader is being willing to change and grow. If you use the information and tools in this chapter, you can develop the type of resilience that can get your company through any difficulty, no matter how daunting.

Key Takeaways

1. Psychological resilience is something that can be cultivated if you work at it.
2. A great leader cannot force resilience upon subordinates, but they can model resilient behavior for them.

3. You can develop perspective by cultivating a growth mindset.

4. Letting go of past resentments can help you accept adversity in a strong way instead of thinking like a victim.

5. Getting outside of the leadership bubble is essential if you want to learn how to accept reality.

6. Learning to identify the things you can and can't control is a key component of resilience.

7. Resilient people know when to accept help.

7
The Psychology of Emotional Intelligence

In a very real sense we have two minds, one that thinks and one that feels.

~ Daniel Goleman

When it comes to measuring our abilities and intelligence, we tend to think of IQ tests and scores. As important as these are, they fail to take into account the importance of emotional intelligence, an aspect of intelligence that is one of the most important for leaders.

What Is Emotional Intelligence?

Psychologist Daniel Goleman defined Emotional Intelligence in his landmark book, <u>Emotional Intelligence: Why It Can Matter More Than IQ</u>,[1] as having four basic areas:

1. **Self-awareness** consisting of three separate elements. First, the awareness of your own emotions as emotions. This means being able to recognize when you feel angry, sad, and so on. Second, the ability to

accurately assess your own emotions and skills. And third, self-confidence, which comes from knowing who you are and believing that you have the ability to deal with situations as they arise.

2. **Self-management** involves having the ability to control your own behavior in a variety of ways. This involves general emotional control—the ability to rein in emotions when necessary and appropriate. Other traits that fall into this category include trustworthiness, reliability, adaptability, conscientiousness, being achievement oriented, and taking initiative.

3. **Social awareness** involves your emotional awareness of the people around you, including empathy toward others, awareness of any organizations or groups of which you are a part, and the ability to orient yourself in service to other people or a cause.

4. **Relationship management** encompasses your ability to interact, and build relationships, with other people. It includes skills such as team-building, communication, conflict management, inspiring others, building bonds with other people, and being a catalyst for change.

True emotional intelligence requires a leader to have nine or ten core competencies that span all four of the above areas.

Why Emotional Intelligence Matters

Why does emotional intelligence matter? When it comes to leadership and professional success, many leaders value their innate intelligence and level of education more than their ability to accurately assess and control their own emotions or to work well with others. However, the opposite is actually true. People with high IQs tend to outperform those with average IQs only about 20% of the time. However, people with higher emotional intelligence tend to outperform those with lower emotional intelligence 70% of the time.[2]

When psychologist Jennifer M. George studied how emotions affect leadership, she found that both positive and negative emotions, as well as a leader's awareness of them, help improve leadership.[3] One example she uses is that of a leader who learns that a covert pattern of sexual harassment exists in the organization. The leader's emotional intelligence helped them resolve this situation because they were able to control their anger to stimulate them to take decisive action.

In order to better understand the importance of emotional intelligence, let's look at some additional studies.

- A 2001 study showed that the emotions of leaders are contagious, spread easily to employees and can affect employee productivity—as well as the company's bottom line.[4] In fact, an upbeat attitude from management was found to foster optimism and creativity in employees.

- Studies have found a direct link between emotional intelligence and employee performance and business profit. For example, a 2015 study found that companies whose employees rated their leaders highly in terms of their compassion, forgiveness, integrity and responsibility performed almost five times better than those whose leaders received low ratings in these areas.[5] And a 2005 study revealed that emotionally intelligent leaders were far more likely to elicit a high level of performance from their employees than leaders who lacked emotional intelligence.[6]

- A 2010 study by Gilkey, Caceda and Kilts showed that people with great emotional intelligence tend to be better strategic thinkers than those who lack emotional intelligence.[7]

- Leaders who have emotional intelligence tend to be more creative than those who do not. They are also more likely to be able to inspire cooperation in their employees and to recognize how their own emotions, both negative and positive, will impact their judgment.[8]

- Self-control is a key component of emotional intelligence. An examination of people whose careers faltered revealed that those who demonstrated high levels of self-control and restraint were far more likely to be successful than those who did not.[9]

These studies demonstrate that emotional intelligence is an indispensable quality of great leaders. In fact, psychologist Reldan S. Nadler points out that as leaders advance, their individual skills diminish in importance while their ability to build teams and manage others increases in importance.[10] Those skills have little to do with IQ and everything to do with emotional intelligence.

Qualities of Ineffective Leadership

If emotional intelligence is essential to good leadership, how can a lack of emotional intelligence hurt leaders and organizations? In her book <u>The EQ Difference</u>, author Adele B. Lynn asked a group of people to describe the qualities of the worst bosses they ever had.[11] Responses included:

- Poor communication skills
- Micromanagement
- Insensitivity
- Being temperamental
- Belittling
- Negativity
- Being unapproachable
- Blaming

Collectively, her survey group told her that working for someone who demonstrated a lack of emotional intelligence made them feel anxious, trapped, worthless, unmotivated, and demoralized—supporting the conclusion that emotional intelligence is critical for all leaders.

Using Emotional Intelligence to Succeed

In Nadler's 2011 book <u>Leading with Emotional Intelligence</u>, he profiles Mark French, a former coach of the women's basketball team at the University of California, Santa Barbara.[12] French is referred to as the 'Legend of the Dome' because of his impressive leadership resulting in his team winning 12 straight Big West titles. French's success is thought to be attributed to a number of key actions, including:

- Acknowledging that success is mostly mental and emotional—96% of French's coaching does not involve time spent playing basketball.
- Placing a high importance on *preparation* (practice) instead of on performance—the opposite of what usually happens in the world of business.
- Encouraging team bonding.
- Building open relationships with all players and mentoring them as needed.
- Knowing his players' individual strengths and weaknesses.

- Spending time with each player one-on-one.
- Giving feedback in a timely manner.
- Taking responsibility for his own mistakes when the team does not succeed.

All of these skills demonstrate emotional intelligence and are applicable in business leadership.

Case Study – Jeff Bezos of Amazon.com

Jeff Bezos of internet giant Amazon.com is an admired leader. He took an idea that seemed revolutionary when it first came on the scene—selling books online—and turned it into one of the world's largest and most successful companies. While his intelligence and business savvy were certainly important, there is also evidence to suggest that emotional intelligence has played a big role in his success.

Bezos' approach to customer experience is a clear example of his social awareness and relationship management—key components of emotional intelligence.[13] In every meeting he conducts at Amazon, Bezos sets an empty chair. He tells employees that the empty chair is for the meeting's most important participant—the customer—a symbol possibly to show that the customer is important and is to be considered.

This commitment to customer service—and a focus on customer emotions and needs–looms large at Amazon. The company uses over 500 metrics to measure performance, and at least 80% of them relate to customer experience. Bezos' focus pushes his employees to place themselves in the customer's shoes, and has led to innovations such as same-day delivery and even the invention of the now-famous Kindle e-reader.

It is important to note that there are areas where Bezos' approach could be further adapted. His focus on customers is great for business, but it has also led many to rate Amazon as a stressful work environment. As a result, the company has fairly high turnover.[14] The key takeaway here is that it is just as important for leaders to understand employees' emotions as it is to understand those of their customers.

Lessons for Leaders

Here are some practical tools to help you and leaders in your organization to apply the key psychological principles of emotional intelligence.

- **Development tools**. The GENOS Emotional Intelligence Inventory is a tool that looks at the presence of 70 different emotionally intelligent behaviors in the workplace.[15] Primarily intended as a tool for Human Resource professionals, it can be used as a self-assessment to assess your emotional intelligence and help you to identify areas for improvement. It looks at these seven basic categories of behavior:

- Emotional self-awareness
- Emotional expression
- Emotional awareness of others
- Emotional reasoning
- Emotional self-management
- Emotional management of others
- Emotional self-control

There are many tools to assess emotional intelligence on the market that can be used for leadership development. The key point is that enhancing self-awareness is the critical first step before encouraging change.

- **Reflection and self-evaluation.** Consider what types of emotions you tend to experience at work and situations that typically cause them. Are these emotions beneficial or detrimental? Identify the detrimental emotions and the triggers that bring these emotions on. Reflect and learn as much as you can about these situations and consider what you could do differently to decrease the impact or occurrence of your triggers.

- **Label emotions.** When you experience emotions, label them. Neuroscience has shown that labeling your emotions *accurately* reduces their impact. However, most people's emotional vocabulary is quite limited. To improve this, it might help to download and study a list of emotions. For example, there are many nuanced emotions related to 'anger': irritation, bitterness, sharpness, enviousness, and so forth. The wider your vocabulary, the more effective this strategy will be.

- **Seek feedback.** Feedback is an integral part of learning and can give you insight into your blind spots and how other people perceive you. Feedback is neither right nor wrong. It is the perception of another party, and knowing their view can allow you to do something about it. You do not have to agree with the feedback, but try not to refute it, justify, or make excuses. These reactions will impact the likelihood of this person giving you honest feedback in the future. Simply listen, reflect and thank the person for their honesty. Acknowledge the positive and constructive comments. It is very easy to hone in on the negative comments and forget the positive remarks. More information on the psychological principles of feedback is covered later in chapter 12.

Applications for Your Organization

Here are some practical organization-wide tools that have worked for other companies and assisted in building a culture of emotional intelligence:

- **Measure emotional intelligence when hiring.** Most companies tend to focus on functional (skill-based) leadership instead of on ability leadership. When recruiting, consider the difficulty in training skills such as emotional intelligence, and recruit for this. Functional skills can be learned. To do this you can utilize an emotional intelligence psychometric assessment—just be sure to check the validity and reliability of the tool before using it. You can also assess emotional-intelligence traits such as self-awareness through interview and reference-check questions. For example, you could ask a question such as, 'Could you tell me about a time you got tough feedback from your boss?' This question can help you to gain insight into the applicant's self-awareness, confidence, open mindedness, and ability to receive and utilize critical feedback.

- **Educate your teams about emotional intelligence and reward high emotional intelligence.** Use emotional intelligence to build effective teams and foster team efficiency. The key components to building transformational teamwork is trust among team members, a sense of group identity, and a sense of group efficacy.[16] The only way to create such an atmosphere is to focus on the emotions and responses of team members, both as individuals and collectively. Do this by encouraging open and honest communication, fostering a sense of camaraderie, and building morale. Make sure that the team has a sense of how its work and emotions affect other individuals and teams.

- **Communicate effectively and respectfully.** Communication is key to emotionally intelligent practices. Leaders must be able to communicate effectively and to encourage effective and respectful communication among team members.[17] The best way to do that is to focus on four key aspects of communication:
    - Why team members need to communicate with one another
    - What form their communication takes
    - The content of the communication, both verbal and non-verbal—it is important that the group has a common language
    - The roles of the communicators, both sender and receiver

It is important that the team environment is a safe environment where team members are encouraged and supported to speak up when they feel that the group is not being productive. Emotionally intelligent teams face potentially difficult information and actively seek opinions.

It is also important that an affirmative environment is created where challenges are faced with a can-do attitude. This doesn't always come naturally to a team, and so it is important for leaders to model the desired behaviors. When there is a cycle of negativity among the group, disrupt the cycle and resist the temptation to contribute. Instead encourage a proactive problem-solving approach and focus on what is within the group's control.

By ensuring that team members learn and use effective communication skills—and by demonstrating those skills on a regular basis—leaders can improve teamwork and foster an emotionally intelligent environment in which work is done as efficiently, and with as little stress, as possible.

- **Build emotionally intelligent norms.** It is important for teams to establish a group identity and norms that support emotionally intelligent practices. Norms are the attitudes and behaviors that eventually become habits. These norms must be reinforced over and over again. When values and norms are clear, and self-management principles are explicit, teams become more likely to hold each other accountable for sticking to norms. More information on the psychological principles for building effective teams is covered later in chapter 14.

- **Motivate.** Emotional intelligence enables effective leaders to motivate their employees to do good work. All motivation begins with one of two questions. Either, "What's in it for me?" or, "What's in it for my team?"[18] As a leader, look at the needs and desires of your team members as individuals *and* of your team as a whole and use that information as a way of providing them with motivation. The key is to understand that motivation is inherently emotional. You can motivate employees by soliciting their opinions about how the team could be more productive, sharing what you learn in team meetings, and providing some concrete incentives that will reward the team's performance if they are successful.

The bottom line is that emotional intelligence can do a great deal to elicit good results both from you and your employees. If you use the tools outlined above, you will be able to manage your own emotions and use your understanding of your employees' feelings to be a more effective leader.

Key Takeaways

1. Emotional intelligence breaks down into four categories: self-awareness, self-management, social awareness, and relationship management.
2. People who are emotionally intelligent tend to outperform those who have high IQs but low emotional intelligence about 70% of the time. Furthermore, companies whose leaders are emotionally intelligent outperform other companies when it comes to seeing a return on their assets.
3. Research shows that emotional intelligence grows in importance as leaders move up the ladder.
4. Effective leaders demonstrate emotional intelligence by emphasizing preparation, encouraging team bonding, building relationships, knowing their employees' strengths and weaknesses, providing feedback, and taking responsibility for their own actions.
5. Ineffective leaders lack emotional intelligence and tend to be insensitive, temperamental, unapproachable, and poor communicators.

6. Emotionally intelligent leaders have the ability to inspire transformation both in their employees and in their organizations.

7. There is a direct link between the ability to control one's emotions and individual success.

8. Assessment tools such as the GENOS Emotional Intelligence Inventory can help leaders assess their own emotional intelligence and identify areas where they might need to improve.

9. Emotionally intelligent leaders can strengthen their teams by building trust, group identity, and a sense of group efficacy.

10. Demonstrating emotional intelligence results in a high level of job performance and job satisfaction for employees.

11. Emotionally intelligent leaders demonstrate and encourage effective communication from all angles.

12. Emotional intelligence allows leaders to motivate employees both as individuals and as part of a team.

8
The Psychology of Motivation

Motivation is everything. You can do the work of two people, but you can't be two people. Instead, you have to inspire the next guy down the line and get him to inspire his people.

~ Lee Iacocca

For good reason, every great battle scene on stage or screen begins with a rousing speech. When leaders request difficult things from their followers, they must provide motivation if they hope to get results. Speeches are an easy way to dramatize motivation; in real life, motivation can take many different forms.

What Is Motivation?

Psychologist Abraham Maslow defined motivation as something driven by what he called the hierarchy of needs.[1] Maslow proposed that motivation is driven by need—and that basic needs must be met before any person can be motivated to work toward attaining higher needs. For example, a person who is starving is lacking the basic need for food. Before that person can be motivated to worry about their happiness or even their own safety, they must first fulfill the basic need for food.

The hierarchy of needs breaks down into five sections:

- Basic needs including food, water, and shelter. In a work context, this looks like earning enough salary to pay the bills and feed the family.
- Safety needs including protecting the body, income, family, property, and health.
- Love and belonging needs including friendship, family, relationships and feeling part of a team.
- Esteem needs including self-respect, confidence, achievement, and respect by and of others
- Self-actualization, including creativity, morality, spontaneity, problem-solving, lack of prejudice, and acceptance of facts.

This hierarchy is often depicted as a pyramid with basic needs at the bottom and self-actualization needs at the top. Another way to think of motivation is that it is driven by self-interest first. Only when a person feels that their basic needs of survival and safety are met are they capable of looking beyond themselves and serving a greater good.

Why Motivation is so Important

Some leaders make the mistake of thinking that monetary compensation is sufficient to motivate their employees. However, assuming that employees' basic needs of survival are met, employees require other kinds of meaning to be motivated at work.[2] For instance:

- Employees who feel vested in the outcome of their work are more likely to perform well than those who do not. For that reason, intrinsic motivation (motivation driven by interest, curiosity, and investment) can be more powerful than extrinsic motivation (motivation driven by gain or the threat of punishment).[3]

- Motivation for groups helps to drive performance, as well as the perceived status, of members within the group.[4] The ability of employees to work efficiently in teams is essential to any organization's success, and a properly motivated group is likely to reward even members who lack external status.

- A lack of motivation can increase employees' anxiety and negative reactions to mistakes.[5] Conversely, employees who are properly motivated are likely to take mistakes in stride and keep negative emotions in check, both of which can positively affect the performance of an entire organization.

- Research indicates that leaders with a strong sense of motivation tend to outperform other leaders who lack motivation.[6]

Overall, a motivated workforce can mean the difference between employees wanting to be at work and being productive, and employees dreading work and being inefficient. In my experience a large percentage of poor-performance cases are a result of low motivation.

The Psychological Principles of Motivation

Let's look at what the research says about intrinsic and extrinsic motivational strategies and the most effective ways to motivate employees at work.

Extrinsic Factors

Early approaches to motivation concentrated on extrinsic factors. That is, motivators which come by way of either reward or punishment. Behavioral psychologist B.F. Skinner[7] popularized this line of research. Skinner would store mice inside a chamber with an electrified floor. To punish certain behaviors, he would stun the mice with an electric shock. To reward behavior, he would supply the mice with a food pellet. It worked! Skinner could successfully manipulate the behavior of these mice using simple reward or punishment.

However, human beings aren't mice. We can't just point to the work of early behaviorists and say, "See, if we want Jim to work harder we just need to provide sufficient reward, or punishment, or both!" This is the carrot and the stick approach.

Of course, rewards and punishment can work on humans. They can be used to get people to do things. But those people won't necessarily want to do what they are being told. And really, to what standard, and for how long, will somebody do something they don't want to do? That's the limitation of extrinsic motivators. The solution? Employ motivating factors which are intrinsic in nature. Human beings are complex and so this means when shaping (or directing) behavior, one must consider feelings, personality, prior experience, mood, beliefs, etc.

Intrinsic Factors

Intrinsic motivation can be broken down into:

1. **Philosophy/spiritualism/values.** A person can be motivated to do something if the request aligns with their values or philosophical or spiritual beliefs. Not because they're paid or threatened, but because they feel it's the right thing to do.

    For example, consider the Japanese. Modern Japanese culture was shaped during the Edo period, between 1603 and 1868. When defining the social norms, the ruling power expected people to live by, they borrowed heavily from principles of Confucianism. At the core of Confucianism is the philosophy that one is to work toward the greater good. It's collective rather than individualistic. As such, responsibility falls to the individual to be the very best they can be. To aspire for perfection because the better each individual is, the better we all are. Deeply ingrained in Japanese culture is a dedication to the perfection of their craft; not for money or survival, but because it is part of their intrinsic philosophy, their belief system.[8]

2. **Inherent interest/joy.** In 1949, psychologist Harry F. Harlow took a group of rhesus monkeys and gave them a puzzle to solve.[9] After two weeks, these monkeys were completing the puzzle in less than 60 seconds. Not once did these monkeys receive food, affection, or any other token reward for completing the puzzle. They did it only, from all accounts, out of sheer enjoyment.

If these monkeys performed so well purely driven by interest, wouldn't you expect them to perform even better if a reward was presented? That's what Dr. Harlow tested, and what he found was quite remarkable. Results showed the introduction of a reward (raisins) actually *decreased* performance. The monkeys made significantly more errors, and completion rates dropped.

It took another twenty years for two graduates from Carnegie Mellon University and The Wharton School of the University of Pennsylvania to test Harlow's findings on human participants. They found rewards (money) increased performance, but only over the short term. Over time, the effects would wear off and performance would drop below previous standards and remain there.[10] The introduction of a reward appeared to dissolve the inherent interest that was previously driving performance. This is known as the *overjustification effect*.

Open source computer programming is another great example of inherent interest. Open source programmers don't get paid and they don't get recognition. Yet they dedicate a tremendous amount of their time, often toward projects that will only ever serve a handful of users. So why do they do it? In a joint study between MIT Sloan School of Management and The Boston Consulting Group, researchers looked into the motivation of open source programmers. They concluded, "... that enjoyment-based intrinsic motivation, namely how creative a person feels when working on the project, is the strongest and most pervasive driver."[11]

This is not to say people will work for free. They won't. But it should compel you to seek additional and complementary means for motivating your team. Particularly if you are asking them to undertake a creative or problem-solving task, because this is where external rewards can stifle performance the most.

Ask yourself how you could align employees' job tasks with their existing belief systems. Or, how you could make their day-to-day experiences inherently more interesting? What motivates your employee? (Remember, it is they who define "interesting," not you).

Changing needs

Another interesting aspect of motivation is the way people's motivational needs change as they age. In the paper, *Aging, Adult Development, and Work Motivation*, Ruth Kanfer and Phillip L. Ackerman looked at workplace motivation as it relates to people over the age of 50. What they found is that older people tend to be more motivated by cooperation and teamwork than by outright competition.[12] Their research demonstrated that as we age our motivations can change, thus creating another dynamic for organizations to consider.

The key takeaway from motivational research is that motivation is a key factor for eliciting performance from employees, and that different forms of motivation can motivate different people. For organizations, this means being adaptive and ever evolving. So, let's look at how different organizations successfully do this, starting with an example from Volkswagen.

Motivation in Action - Volkswagen

Volkswagen wanted to find a way to motivate more people to drive environmentally-friendly cars, and came up with the hypothesis that people would be more inclined to do the right thing if it was also fun.[13] They asked people to find ways to encourage healthy or responsible behavior through fun. One of the most interesting examples took place at a subway station in Stockholm, Sweden. Here they observed through hidden cameras people's preference to take the escalator over the healthy option of the stairs. However, when workers turned the stairs into a working piano—increasing the fun— usage of the staircase increased 66%.

In this example, Volkswagen employees used the disguise of fun to enhance motivation. So this became the practice adopted, by incentivizing workers with contests or finding ways to turn work into play in order to improve productivity and performance.

Motivation in Action – Walt Disney

Another example of motivation in practice is Walt Disney. Walt Disney's company became as successful as it is in part because he excelled at motivating his employees in a way that incorporated both financial motivation and fun. Perhaps nowhere is his style better illustrated than in the story of how Disneyland expanded its hours.[14]

Walt wanted more money to make movies. However, he was unable to get his brother, who was in charge of the company's purse strings, to give it to him. He pulled together a team of seven people and asked if they could find ways to get more money out of the park. One of the team members took out a calendar and pointed out that the park wasn't open on Mondays and Tuesdays—why not open it? Walt was reluctant, but the team came up with the idea of forming a Magic Kingdom Club that would let their corporate members give employees discounted tickets on those days.

It was a huge success, and on Christmas Day, those employees opened their doors to find Mickey Mouse standing there with $25,000 in cash, 100 shares of Disney stock, and a handwritten note from Walt himself that included these four words: "Let's do it again."

The motivation worked. When Disney asked them to do it again, the same team came up with the idea of keeping the park open late on Thursday and calling it Grad Nights to appeal to seniors who were graduating from high school. He repeated the same thank you, but added a Ferrari to the bonus.

What can leaders learn from Walt Disney's example?

1. The first thing he did was present employees with a problem—how to make more money from Disneyland.
2. Importantly, he asked his employees to be part of the solution and he gave them the opportunity to do so.
3. When they came up with an idea he pushed them to refine it.
4. And when it succeeded, he rewarded them in a way that was generous, fun, and personal. (After all, he could have simply presented them with the check and the shares in the office.)

Thus, armed with the knowledge that hard work and innovation would be rewarded, it was extremely unlikely that any one of those seven employees would turn down his request to "do it again." They knew that their work and creativity would be rewarded.

Using Psychological Principles to Motivate Your Employees

Let's look at some specific principles that you can use to help motivate and encourage your employees to do their best work.

- **Survival and safety.** When a person's basic needs of survival and safety have been met, emotion is the single strongest driver of motivation.[15] This means that, as a leader, you should find ways to engage your employees' emotions. Encourage a sense of safety and security by letting employees know you appreciate their contributions. Model and support a culture of learning where mistakes are learned from and employees are encouraged to try, to learn, and to try again.

    You cannot build your employee's self-esteem by berating them, or diluting positive feedback by complimenting everything they do. Instead, offers of praise and constructive criticism are equally important. If someone does not meet your expectations, explain how they can do better in the future.

    Because people are different, start with the basic needs first and then build up. Ask people what would motivate them and focus on influencing positive emotions.

- **Job design**. The way a job is designed can have a significant impact on the motivation of employees.[16] There are several applicable theories of job design. A process that works well for repetitive jobs, where boredom may create dysfunctional outcomes, is job rotation. However, for employees who work in groups where both individuals and the group have some degree of autonomy and employees are encouraged to work on their own, socio-technical systems, which rely on goal-directed behavior, work best.

- **Goal-setting**. Encourage employees to set and pursue positive goals for themselves—and to write about those goals. This can be a very effective way of motivating employees to achieve the goals set.[17] More information on using psychology to enhance goal setting can be found in the following chapter.

- **Reward and recognition**. In addition to basic physical and psychological needs, human beings also have a strong need for recognition.[18] Think of the Walt Disney example, and then consider what you can do to provide recognition for your employees. Simple things such as announcing employee accomplishments, or having a monthly "employee recognition" meeting, can work well to motivate employees.

The key to recognition, however, is to recognize day to day achievements. Recognition does not need to be formal or ceremonious. Instead, acknowledge desired behaviors and practices in the workplace. Remember, one of the simplest recognitions is a sincere thank you.

The key is to offer rewards that people desire. Rewards need to be ethical and fairly allocated, and a clear understanding of the criteria for receiving rewards is necessary. Also, don't promise more than you can deliver, be sure to follow through, and use rewards to motivate rather than manipulate. There are various ways to reward staff, including giving more autonomy to employees where earned, involving them in special projects, inviting them to meetings of interest, providing them with training opportunities, and more.

- **Reward learning and positive thinking.** Mindset plays a significant role in motivation. People who have a fixed mindset, such as, "don't make mistakes," or, "don't fail," tend to have relatively poor motivation. Conversely, those who have a growth mindset, geared toward learning new things, tend to have great motivation because they believe they can improve.[19] Leaders can provide motivation by creating an environment in which, first, learning, growth, and creativity are valued, and second, failure is not punished so long as that failure is learned from and the same mistakes are not repeated.

- **Link personality and motivation.**[20] Some people respond best to positive stimuli, such as rewards and recognition, while others are kept motivated by personal projects and articulated goals. Approaching motivation with a "one size fits all" mentality is a mistake. Instead, meet with employees individually, observe them, and provide them with the motivation that will best suit their personalities.

The key to motivating employees is to determine which form of motivation is best suited for your employees both as individuals and as a group, not relying solely on the carrot and the stick, and then providing adaptive motivational strategies targeted to your employees.

Key Takeaways

1. Motivation is based on a hierarchy of needs—only when a person's basic needs of survival and safety are met are they capable of aspiring to loftier goals.

2. People are hardwired to respond to fun. They are more likely to do the right or healthy thing when there is fun involved than they would be in a situation where fun is absent.

3. Most employees need motivation beyond money. As long as their basic needs are met, you must provide them with something more if you want them to succeed.

4. There is a direct link between motivation and success. Both leaders and employees who are motivated are far more likely to succeed than those who lack motivation.

5. Intrinsic motivation is more likely to foster success than extrinsic motivation.

6. Emotion and motivation are directly linked. If you can find a way to make your employees attach emotional importance to their jobs, they will be more motivated than they would be without it.

7. Do what you can to design jobs with motivation in mind. For example, repetitive jobs can be rotated to decrease boredom, while working in autonomous groups can help motivate some employees.

8. Encourage employees to articulate and write about positive goals to help them stay motivated.

9. Establish a growth mindset in the workplace. Employees who know you value creativity, risk-taking, and learning (and do not punish people who have ideas that don't work) will be highly motivated to succeed.

10. When necessary, individualize the motivational techniques you use to match up with employees' personalities.

9
How to Use Psychology to Enhance Goal Setting

What you get by achieving your goals is not as important as what you become by achieving your goals.
~ Zig Ziglar

While there are many qualities that a great leader must possess, one of the most important is the ability to set goals, for oneself as much as for subordinates. Without goals, an organization can end up drifting aimlessly, never achieving much of anything. With them, tremendous things are possible. Goal setting might appear to be a very personal thing. Nevertheless, a leader can formulate department- or company-wide goals and do what is necessary to get their employees to adopt those goals as their own.

Goals... what are those again?

In sporting events, a goal is easy to define. To reach the finish line or score points, a specific series of actions must be taken.

In business and in life, goals tend to be a bit more nebulous. This is particularly true of large, long-term goals, which can be composed of dozens, or even hundreds, of intermediary steps.

A goal is an aim or an envisioned result, and goal setting is the process of identifying a goal and establishing measurable timeframes and actions to achieve it.

The Importance of Goals

Goal setting plays an important role in motivating employees to do their best. An 11-year study published in *Psychological Bulletin* showed that people who had challenging goals performed better than those who had easy or no goals.[1] That conclusion held true for 90% of the study's subjects.

Some of the specific benefits of having challenging goals included:

- Improved attention
- Increased effort
- A higher level of persistence
- Adoption of better strategies

Perhaps the most interesting thing about the study is that in all cases, when the subjects who had been assigned a goal were also provided with regular support and encouragement, they all willingly accepted the goal. In other words, the subjects performed well in the presence of solid leadership related to the attainment of the goals.

Another study in 2005 looked at participants' pursuit of goals as it related to their mental conditioning before they were assigned tasks.[2] What the study found is that the subjects performed more efficiently and effectively when they were primed with positive evaluative conditioning than when they received no conditioning or negative conditioning. This indicated—not surprisingly—that people tend to perform better when they have the following things:

1. A challenging goal for which they have adequate training and strong support; and
2. A positive mindset about the pursuit of the goal in question.

As a leader, effective goal setting enables you to get more out of employees through increased performance, effort, attention, motivation, persistence, and better use of resources. On the other hand, ineffective goal setting can be very destructive. This then begs the question, "What is the most effective way to set and deliver goals?"

The Path-Goal Theory

One of the best-known theories regarding the application of goal setting is the path-goal theory, which was first described by Robert House in 1971. It says that a leader's behavior has a direct impact on the motivation, performance, and satisfaction of subordinates.[3] It is an adaptive leadership theory that assumes that an effective leader can modify their behavior based on the specifics of a situation. They do whatever is necessary to both define goals for subordinates and clear the path of potential obstructions. The theory was later updated to include a statement that a leader's job is to compensate for their subordinates' deficiencies and complement their abilities.[4]

The path-goal theory breaks down into four different types of goal setting, based on both the nature of the goals being pursued and the intrinsic strengths and abilities of the people pursuing them. They are:

1. **Achievement-oriented leader behavior** involves a leader setting challenging goals and expecting their followers to achieve them. A good leader will also provide necessary guidance, but a high standard for both the leader and subordinates is the norm. This version of path-goal theory tends to work best when

there are complex tasks involved that require a high degree of competence.[6]

2. **Participative leader behavior** involves a leader consulting with their subordinates prior to making decisions. This variation of path-goal theory tends to work best when the leader's subordinates have a level of expertise that is required to complete goals, and where they specifically expect to be consulted about goal setting.[7]

3. **Supportive leader behavior** involves a leader expressing concern for their subordinates' psychological well-being, and taking care to create a positive and beneficial work environment. This form of path-goal theory works best when subordinates' jobs are dangerous, stressful, or boring.[8]

4. **Directive leader behavior** involves a leader telling their subordinate what to do and how to do it. This iteration of path-goal theory tends to work best for subordinates who are being asked to do something new or that they may not have done before. A leader using this method will set clear deadlines and benchmarks, and hand out rewards when appropriate.[5]

The key to path-goal theory is being flexible in identifying the need for each potential iteration of the theory and then putting the right type of goal setting in place for the individual, group, or team. A leader in charge of a department will typically find, for example, that participative leader behavior is best for high-level employees, and that directive behavior is necessary for low-level employees who need a lot of guidance to meet goals.

The trick for any leader is also to clarify one's own goals—as well as organizational goals—and then be able to translate them into goals for individual employees. At the same time, leaders must deliver goals in a way that matches the needs of individuals, as well as provide the guidance necessary to ensure that employees can meet the goals laid out for them.

Case Study – Say Yes to Education

To illustrate how the goal-path process works in the real world, let's look at an example. While the company here is a non-profit organization, the lessons they learned can apply to any company in any sector.

Say Yes to Education is a non-profit organization in Harlem that promises a college education to students from poor families if they finish high school. They assign teams to students to help them meet specific goals.

When the company's president pushed his teams to perform better on certain, measurable goals, they pushed back.[9] For every suggestion he made, they had an excuse for why it wouldn't work—more time with the students would mean less time with the parents, and so on.

Finally, he hit on a solution that utilized path-goal theory. Instead of demanding certain goals from them, he turned the goal setting over to his employees, requiring each team to come up with a single result-oriented goal that they could meet in 100 days. This is an example of the participative leader behavior iteration of path-goal theory, and it worked like a charm. The team leaders got creative with goals, doing things like raising children's reading scores by one grade level, and helping parents who were learning English as a second language to improve their fluency.

The takeaway is that the president of Say Yes to Education adapted his approach according to employees' needs and level of competence. He helped them to set achievable goals to ensure that institutional goals were also met. Employees were also accountable for delivering on the goal set—helping with their motivation to follow through.

How to Use Path-Goal Theory

Let's look at some specific ways that you can put path-goal theory to work for you.

Set Institutional and Departmental Goals

The first step in setting goals is to take a big-picture view and then set goals for your company or department. No leader can expect to set realistic goals for their subordinates if they do not have overarching goals for their organization. In a functional hierarchy, each small goal contributes to the large ones.

With that in mind, take some time to define your major goals for the institution or department you lead. Then break down each large goal into small tasks. The more thorough you are at this stage, the easier it will be for you to implement path-goal theory later.

Determine the Best Variation

The next step is to determine the appropriate variation of path-goal theory to use when setting goals for your employees—or helping them set them for themselves. Remember that it is probable that you will need to implement more than one iteration of the theory to cover all of your employees. You will have to look at each employee and determine which process will be the most effective. For medium to large organizations, you certainly cannot do this with all employees in the organization, so focus on your subordinates and then educate and encourage your leadership group to do the same with their subordinates.

The specifics vary from company to company, but here are some basic guidelines you can use:

- For administrative tasks that support a large, complex goal, you should consider the *directive* path-goal option.
- For slightly more technical or complex tasks, an *achievement-oriented* path-goal is the best choice.
- For high-level employees who expect their voices to be heard, use *participative* leader behavior.
- Finally, for employees whose jobs entail a high degree of risk or emotional stress, use *supportive* leader behavior to ensure that employees feel safe and supported.

A good rule of thumb is to start with the highest level tasks (those that require participative behavior) and work your way down. The reason for starting there is that elements will likely come out in your meetings with high-level employees that will help you set goals for those at a lower level.

Suggestions for Implementing Path-Goal Theory

After you have determined which employees will be performing each individual task, start implementing whichever method you will be using. As previously stated, it is best to start at the top with the participative meetings with high-level subordinates.

- **With high-level employees**, make sure to approach the subject of goal-setting with some degree of modesty. It is likely that your leadership group fall into this category. With high-level employees, be careful to ensure that they feel they have been heard and that each employee understands that setting goals is a requirement. Make note of any goals that are set and then establish a system for following up on progress. For high-level employees, a self-reporting system is the best option.

- **For intermediate but relatively self-sufficient employees**, use the achievement-oriented path goal. A good way to approach this is to gather employees and present them with the goals as a challenge. Make sure to emphasize that you have high expectations. Just as you did with the high level employees, make sure that you make it clear which goal belongs to which employee, and determine how and when you will follow up on their progress.

- **For low-level employees** who require a lot of guidance, implement the directive path-goal behavior. Clearly delineate the goals for each employee, and make deadlines and expectations clear. You should also let employees know that stretch goals will be rewarded when it is appropriate. Just as the earlier topic of modesty came into play with high level employees, here you will need to straddle the line between being authoritative and modest.

- **For employees whose jobs entail a high degree of risk or stress** (and it is likely that employees in the above mentioned categories will fall here from time to time)—you also need to bring in supportive path-goal behavior to help them. Remember that risk is not just physical risk. Other examples of risk are emergency medicine, or an organization that deals with at-risk youth. The potential for employee stress and burnout in such situations is very high, and it must be addressed if you want your employees to reach their goals. You need to combine supportive behavior with any (or all) of the other three behaviors to get the result you want.

The key to using path-goal theory is to identify your goals, and know your employees and what they need to be successful in attaining them. There is no single approach that will suit every employee; as a leader, part of your job is to adapt your approach to best match different employees.

More psychological principles for effective goal setting

There are some interesting psychological studies in addition to path-goal theory. These show results indicating some additional significant factors that influence the success of goal setting. These include:

- **Setting unrealistic goals.** Difficult yet specific goals lead to higher performance than do easy but vague goals.[10] However, evidence also indicates that unrealistic goals that are not achieved result in decreased efficacy and a tendency to set lower and easier performance goals thereafter.[11]

- **Self-efficacy.** Self-efficacy refers to task specific confidence—the conviction that, "I can do this." Self-efficacy has a direct relationship with persistence, effort, and performance. This means that employees with higher self-efficacy in relation to the achievement of a goal are more likely to persist in pursuing the goal, put in more effort, and ultimately succeed.[12]

- **Feedback.** Frese and Zapf[13] identify four key steps for increasing motivation for goal achievement. Their theory states that for work to become personally enhancing and motivating, goals must first be set, and then relevant information to the goals should be systematically sought. The next element, and a critical one, is the need for action planning where a plan should be developed for attaining the goals. Finally, and most importantly, feedback on progress should be sought at various points. This feedback will assist in determining where greater effort may be required, if adjustments to the action plan are needed, or more information needs to be collected. The key takeaway from their research is that feedback should be a continual process for refining goals. This feedback can either be verbal feedback or use other modes of feedback from the organization, such as trends in data.

Lessons for leaders

How do you put this evidence into action? Below are some practical tools and tips to assist you.

- **Set challenging but realistic goals.** Unrealistic goals will hinder motivation, as will goals that are too easy.
- **Be specific.** Goals that are specific and challenging lead to higher performance, whereas vague and easy goals allow employees too much wiggle room to get it wrong, head in the wrong direction, or undeservedly pat themselves on the back. To avoid this, be sure to provide employees with enough detail so you and they start on the same page and move in the same

direction. Clarify what success looks like but let employees with the capability determine the 'how' in achieving the goals.

- **Set SMART goals.** Some elements that are critical for effective goal-setting include specificity, measurability, achievability, relatedness, and deadlines.

- **Explain goals in positive terms.** Why should employees be motivated to achieve the goal? Sell the vision to them and why the goal should be important to them, too.

- **Break goals into smaller chunks.** This tactic tricks your brain into thinking that a large goal is more achievable. Evidence for the positive impact of breaking larger goals into smaller achievable chunks can be found across the board, particularly in sport and defence training. For example, marines who undertake underwater tests, where they need to hold their breath for extended periods of time, perform better when they set mini goals. Mentally striving for "just 5 seconds longer," and then another "5 seconds longer," and so on, is more effective than striving for the whole defined period of time. Try this the next time you exercise. If you have a goal of running a certain distance, when you get tired and think you can run no more say to yourself, "Ok, I will just get to this tree" (or some other reference point ahead of you, if no tree is conveniently located) and focus only on getting to this goal point. Then, when you arrive, tell yourself, "Ok, just a little bit further to this next tree." In the workplace, use this technique by setting mini goals that will result in the achievement of a larger goal. This is particularly effective for subordinates who are feeling overwhelmed by a large project or task.

- **Consider team-based goals.** If cooperation is important in the achievement of specific business goals, consider team-based goals rather than individual goals, which will encourage competition.

- **Encourage employees to participate in goal-setting.** In a recent study, scientists and engineers who were allowed to participate in goal-setting actually set more challenging goals and were more motivated in achieving these goals. Where you can, encourage your staff to contribute to goal setting.

- **Provide ongoing feedback on progress.** When plans need to be adjusted, address it. And, when deadlines are being met and everything is on schedule, provide positive feedback. Both of these will help motivate staff. Avoid repeating negative feedback, as this leads to decreased employee effort.[14] Instead, target the core issue for why the employee(s) is not achieving the desired outcome. Support them and develop a plan with them to address the deficit. For example, training may be required, or they may not have access to information that is needed.

- **Build self-efficacy.** People who believe that they are able to achieve a goal are more likely to persist in achieving the goal and put in more effort. To build self-efficacy in your team, first set a goal and then make sure that employees know what they need to do to attain it. Finally, build their confidence in their ability to achieve the goal. Do this through positive feedback and reiterating to them their past success that will aid them with this new goal.

- **Believe in your staff.** The Pygmalion Effect demonstrates that when leaders have high expectations of their staff *and* demonstrate that they believe that their staff can achieve these expectations, this leads to higher performance. Low expectations, on the other hand, lead to a decrease in performance. This means that when employees feel that expectations are low, or that others do not believe in them, they are more likely to perform at a lower standard. This is a form of a self-fulfilling prophecy. The key message here is to expect a lot from your staff and support them in achieving these high expectations.

Remember, goal attainment leads to higher job satisfaction, which in turn leads to setting more challenging goals and greater motivation to achieve these goals, which leads back to higher job satisfaction—and the cycle continues.

Key Takeaways

1. People with challenging goals tend to perform better than those without goals.

2. Mental preparation for a goal is the key to successful attainment of it.

3. Path-goal theory is an adaptive theory of goal setting that leaders can use to set goals for their employees.

4. Low-level employees tend to respond best to directive path-goal setting with a high level of management support and rewards for a job well done.

5. Intermediate employees are best approached with achievement-oriented path-goal setting, with the knowledge that your expectations are high and must be met.

6. High-level employees will appreciate participative path-goal setting that takes into consideration their opinions, expertise, and concerns.

7. At-risk employees at every level will also require supportive path-goal setting that acknowledges the stresses and risks of their jobs.

8. At every level, it is important to establish a method of follow-up and accountability that everybody understands.

10
How Psychology Can Help You Improve Productivity

The productivity of work is not the responsibility of the worker but of the manager.
~ Peter Drucker

Even for leaders who do a good job of setting goals for their company or department, the attainability and direction of those goals won't matter if the leader is unsure how to manage employee productivity. In any organization, there are roadblocks to productivity—things that, for one reason or another, prevent employees from living up to their potential. It is the job of a leader to remove those roadblocks whenever possible.

Productivity Roadblocks

There are three primary roadblocks to productivity: procrastination, perfectionism, and low self-esteem.

Procrastination

The word "procrastination" has Latin loots. *Crastinus* in Latin means "for tomorrow," while *pro,* we probably all remember from our high school English class, means "forward." In English, we understand procrastination to mean the act of putting something off until tomorrow... or even the day after. Procrastination is psychologically complex and can have many causes. Let's look at a few of the most common:

- **Fear**. In the past, when most people had production-based jobs, fear was less likely a factor. Employees had clear quotas and knew exactly what they had to do to meet expectations. Knowledge-based jobs tend to be less closely defined, and when an employee is constantly bombarded with email and other stimuli, they can feel as though they are under attack. Also, knowledge-based jobs bring increasingly high expectations and fear of getting something wrong. These fears trigger the "fight or flight" response, and adrenaline and cortisol are released into the body. An easy flight response is avoidance, and procrastination offers the short-term reward of helping us dodge a problem. However, this avoidance can very quickly become a pattern of behavior. [1]

- **Feeling overwhelmed**. Another common cause of procrastination is the feeling of being overwhelmed.

Employees most commonly feel overwhelmed due to work volume, work difficulty, information overload, or as a result of emotional factors that may or may not have anything to do with work. A study in 1990 found that both a fear of failure and a fear of success caused procrastination because of feelings of being overwhelmed.[2] More recently, the professional services firm Deloitte conducted research with 2,500 business professionals across 94 countries. They found that 65 percent of executives believe that the stress of being overwhelmed is an urgent and important issue to address. In this research, 72 percent of employees indicated that they "cannot find the information they need within their company's information systems." 41 percent also believed that they spend their time on things that don't satisfy them personally and do not help productivity. All of which result in feelings of being overwhelmed.[3]

- **Instant gratification**. At first glance, the connection between instant gratification and procrastination may not seem obvious. However, employees who crave instant gratification will often have a hard time sticking to long-term goals where the gratification will be delayed. The famous Stanford marshmallow study examined the need for instant gratification and found that it was widespread.[4] The study gave children the choice between having a marshmallow immediately and waiting ten minutes, after which they would be rewarded with a second marshmallow. Few of the children were able to wait. A follow-up study revealed that the children who were able to delay gratification grew into adults who were goal-oriented and productive.[5] This experiment is a classic example of want versus need. Procrastination is all about instant gratification and choosing want over need. Humans are really bad at predicting future mental states—later is a murky place and so the immediate is much easier to deal with. This is what drives procrastination—procrastination is an impulse that takes care of an immediate need.

Perfectionism

Perfectionism can also be a roadblock to productivity. As a leader, you might think that having employees who hold themselves to a high standard is beneficial. And it is. However, if the standard is too high, it can become a problem. Since perfection is not attainable, desiring it can bring productivity to a standstill.

In fact, a 2014 study identified a direct correlation between perfectionism and a lack of problem-solving ability.[6] The problem with perfectionism is that it can freeze creativity and drive. If all an employee can think about is that their work isn't perfect, then they are unlikely to take chances or move forward. Instead, they end up stuck on the same task indefinitely.

Low Self-Esteem

It is perhaps not surprising that low self-esteem can impact productivity. People who are not feeling good about themselves and their abilities often find it difficult to be motivated to keep working.

A 2001 study examined the correlation between productivity and four different factors: self-esteem, self-efficacy, locus of control, and emotional stability. It found a significant correlation between low self-esteem and a lack of employee productivity.[7]

Identifying what is causing a lack of productivity among employees can be tricky, but with or without internal or external help, it is the job of a leader to do exactly that.

Productivity Tools

Overcoming these productivity roadblocks can be a challenge, but there are some tools that can help. Each of these tools addresses the most common roadblocks to productivity and can assist both you and your employees. Below is a list of productivity tools and strategies. Rather than trying to use all of them, adopt a tool for the roadblock you are facing.

1. **Eisenhower's time management matrix**. A valuable first tool to assist with feeling overwhelmed due to having too many tasks is the time management matrix. This will assist in determining which tasks to handle first. Many people spend their time doing things that are not really important, and it can be difficult to prioritize. A simple, four-quadrant matrix can help.[8] The top left quadrant is the 'urgent and important' quadrant. The top right is the 'not urgent but important' quadrant. In the bottom left is the 'urgent but not important' quadrant and in the bottom right is the 'not urgent, not important' quadrant. Use this matrix and encourage your subordinates to use the matrix to categorize tasks. The key to this matrix is that you should be making 'urgent important' tasks a priority. Follow that with the 'important but not urgent' tasks. The 'urgent but not important' tasks should be examined to determine if they are really necessary and should be done after the important tasks. Finally, the 'not urgent, not important' tasks should be eliminated where possible.

2. **The 80-20 rule**. The Pareto Principle states that for many events, roughly 80 percent of effects come from 20 percent of the causes. In a work context, this means that rather than spreading yourself too thin and trying to do everything, you should instead focus your attention on the most important work by identifying the

20 percent of tasks that will provide you with 80 percent of the results.

3. **Chunking tasks**. Chunking works like a cognitive compression mechanism, where we group and order information into chunks that are more memorable and easier to process.[9] As a simple example, suppose that there are two items on a to-do list. One is filing paperwork, and the other is pulling files. Those two tasks are clearly related to one another, in that they both require a trip to the file room. Productivity goes up when the two tasks are chunked together and done one right after the other.

   Chunking can work in the opposite way, too. A big goal that is fairly nebulous can be broken down into small chunks. The larger and more difficult the goal, the more we avoid it. Breaking a large goal into smaller chunks tricks your brain into thinking that this small goal is more achievable and so you are more motivated to get started. When you succeed at this small task, you experience a reward response where your brain releases dopamine (responsible for pleasure and learning). As a result, you feel greater concentration and are inspired to re-experience the activity—in this case, the next small task—that caused the release.

4. **Timing tasks.** The fourth technique you can use to help increase productivity is the Pomodoro Technique.[10] This is a technique that requires using a timer to work without interruption for a defined period of time, most commonly 25 minutes. The theory behind this technique is that it improves focus and productivity by taking some of the pressure off of the person doing the work. Working indefinitely can be difficult, but most of us can put our heads down and work for 25 minutes. The important thing is to decide on an amount of time—typically less than 90 minutes—and set a realistic goal for what you can achieve in that time. Over time, increase the difficulty of the goal that you think you should achieve in this time. This turns your work into a game, where you are driven to achieve what you set out to achieve, in the time you have set. You can then take a short break, set a new goal and off you go again.

5. **Memory tool - thought pad.** There will be times where you are in the middle of a task and a thought, not relevant to what you are doing, will jump out at you. In this moment, it is important to stop, write the thought down immediately and then get back to your task at hand. Once you have finished your task, you can come back to this separate thought. If instead you keep trying to persevere without jotting your thought down, or you try to remember your thought for later,

you impact your ability to focus and your productivity drops because your brain is expending energy trying to store this thought. Writing the side thought down tells your brain that it is okay for you to refocus all of your attention back to the task at hand.

6. **Five minute miracle.** The five minute miracle involves asking yourself, "What action can I spend less than five minutes on TODAY that moves this forward even the tiniest bit?" Once you've identified a small action, set a timer for five minutes and spend that time working on the task. Studies show that once you start something, you're much more likely to finish it. This is due to a psychological phenomenon called the Zeigarnik effect[11], which says that unfinished tasks are more likely to get stuck in your memory. This is why our minds get stuck in a loop thinking about all of the things we haven't yet completed. Remember, small actions are still actions. Five minutes can make all the difference.

7. **Work to your biological clock.** As soon as you arrive at work, spend 30 minutes completing easy action items on your daily task list—only the easy and quick tasks. This will give you a sense of achievement and reward first thing in the morning, and make your task list look much shorter and achievable. Next, do the task for the day that requires the most mental energy.

Most people's brains are at their most alert and best able to focus in the morning. When you experience a lull in energy—for most people, this happens often in the afternoon—schedule routine tasks that you can complete without needing to think too much. When our energy is naturally lower, rather than trying to persevere but be less efficient by working on tasks that require greater mental capacity, work on completing routine tasks that take little creative thought.

8. **Set your environment.**

    a. **Emails**. Schedule set times throughout the day to check your email. Only view your emails when you can respond to them immediately. This saves you time in rereading emails later. Turn off your email noise and visual reminders. If you do not have an executive assistant, or even if you do, use tools such as SaneBox to filter your less important emails and Unrol.Me to compile all of your newsletters into a single email bundle.

    b. **Declutter**. Studies show that excess clutter contributes to stress and anxiety, and makes it more difficult to get work done. Do what you can in your work environment to make the environment clean, organized, focused, and pleasant. For your employees, also consider your business etiquette rules—for example, for noise and file storage.

   c. **Block distractions.** Use tools such as RescueTime to block sites that distract you.

9. **Make meetings count.** A study from the London School of Economics and Harvard Business School showed that most CEOs spend about a third of their time in meetings.[12] That's a lot of valuable time that can be wasted. To make meetings as worthwhile as possible, make sure before the meeting that all attendees know the topic, time, owner, and goal. What are you going to discuss? How long are you going to spend discussing this? Why are you discussing this? What is the ultimate goal of the meeting? Carefully consider who you invite to the meeting. If this is a brainstorming meeting, having too many heads can unnecessarily drag out the process. Having too few, though, risks not achieving what you were hoping to. Ask yourself if a meeting is the best mode for discussing the matter. Is there an agenda to keep everyone on track? What pre-work can be sent that will make the meeting more productive? How long is the meeting scheduled for? Having a culture of setting 50 minute instead of 60 minute meetings can help to combat a workplace culture of people arriving late to meetings. This 10 minutes instead is a gap to

allow people to get to and from meetings that have been scheduled back to back. Starting meetings late is a huge time waster, so don't accept or model this behavior.

Remember:

If you are looking for tools to assist with procrastination, then first try chunking tasks, the 80-20 rule, the five minute miracle, setting goals, and feedback.

For issues with fear, use chunking tasks and key leader qualities such as listening and trust.

For issues with people feeling overwhelmed, use the time management matrix, 80-20 rule, the five minute miracle, chunking tasks, email management, and feedback.

For issues regarding instant gratification, use chunking tasks, timing tasks, and feedback.

For issues with perfectionism, match challenges to skills, lead by example, and provide feedback.

For low self-esteem, use the chunking tasks, listening, trust, and feedback.

For general productivity improvements, listen to your biological clock, use memory tools, set the environment, and make meetings count.

Leading by example, creating the desired culture, flexible work practices, and growing team effectiveness will influence all of the most common productivity roadblocks.

How to Encourage Productivity in Employees

All of the above tools can be used for you and your subordinates. Listed below are some additional techniques that you can use to assist your employees in becoming more productive. Again, this is a long list, so use the tool(s) that will best target the productivity roadblock you are facing.

1. **Lead well, and by example.** Leaders set an example for expected behaviors in an organization. What type of behaviors are you role modeling? There are a few key leadership behaviors that will help you to set the right tone for improving productivity in the workplace, including:

    a. **Listen**. Sometimes, employees just need a chance to share what they are thinking, ask questions, and express their concerns. You need to not only say that you have an open door policy, but follow through with it. This means listening to employee concerns with an open mind, focusing on solutions rather than problems, and guiding employees to find solutions to work problems. This will help to build a more productive work culture.

b. **Provide feedback to employees on a regular basis**. Research shows that simply providing adequate feedback is sufficient to get employees back on track.[14] Regular meetings make it possible for you to provide support and encouragement to subordinates who suffer from low self-esteem. It can also help subordinates stay on track when they are seeking instant gratification, feeling overwhelmed, or behaving like a perfectionist. More information is provided on using psychology to enhance feedback in chapter 12.

c. **Build trust**. Encourage subordinates to come to you when they encounter roadblocks to productivity. If your subordinates are scared to come to you because they fear repercussions, you can rest assured that they won't come to you—and you'll be the last to know when there's a problem. Encourage subordinates to address concerns where they can. When they do come to you with bigger issues, encourage them to come to you with ideas for solutions rather than simply dumping problems. For some things, however, they will look to you for a solution and that is okay, but you want to avoid your office being a room for simply complaining.

2. **Influence the culture of the workplace positively.** Many organizations run by a culture of 'be *seen* to be busy'. This promotes the mentality of 'get in before, and leave after, the boss'. However, this mentality creates a cycle that results in employees working long hours unproductively. Do you want to encourage and reward efficiency and productivity or do you want to reward people who stay late even though they are not doing much at all. You have influence over culture through the setup and governance of the organization, but also through role modeling. If you are in the office before sunrise, stay late every night, and eat lunch at your desk every day, it is likely that your employees will follow your lead and do the same. If you need to work long hours but you don't want to set this precedent, then make a few changes. If you tend to send emails late at night, instead time them to automatically be sent during core business hours. If you need to work late, rather than staying in the office late, use an external working area such as the library or a home office.

3. **Allow flexible work schedules.** While not practical for all businesses, allowing employees some flexibility in when and where they work can go a long way toward increasing productivity. More and more businesses are rewarding employees with remote working, part-time arrangements, and flexible hours, so that employees can manage external responsibilities and bring fewer external distractions into the workplace. This also allows employees to work to their natural body clock when they are most focused and productive. Flexible workplaces can also help you attract high calibre people who otherwise may not apply.

4. **Enhance team effectiveness.** If you have teams that are dysfunctional and do not communicate well, there are bound to be problems with productivity, stress, and conflict. Leaders need to encourage teams to bond with each other and build solid, trusting relationships. When teams are strong, there is greater accountability, better communication, and greater trust. To enhance team productivity, focus on communication. How does the team communicate, with whom, how often, and when? Conflict is a huge time waster, so address it early. Have clear and communicated team rules governing how people should behave, and use team productivity tools such as Asana. More information on building effective teams is provided in chapter 14.

5. **Match challenges to skills.** Employees tend to do best when they have jobs that are challenging but not too far above their pay grade.[15] When you and your managers assign goals and tasks, work to ensure that you do so in a thoughtful way. This means matching employee strengths to tasks, sharing workloads equally, coaching and supporting employees through stretch activities, and providing training to improve skill and knowledge where needed.

6. **Track work for a short period.** Ask subordinates to track their work for a fortnight, a week, or even for a day, depending on the issue at hand. Make clear that asking them to do so is not punitive. Rather, you want to help them increase their productivity. If you notice, for example, that a particular subordinate is spending significant time with external stakeholders and not enough time guiding internal employees, then you can objectively address this by looking at the breakdown of time spent on different activities. The key here is you want to help subordinates identify what tasks they can stop, do more efficiently, or need to put more focus toward.

Every leader wants to have motivated and productive employees. To do that, you need to be a hands-on leader in terms of how you approach productivity. It is true that some employees have the ability to keep themselves motivated and productive at all times. However, most employees face roadblocks to productivity on a daily basis. Some come from within, while others are environmental. Regardless of their origin, it is your job to identify those roadblocks and to give employees the tools and support they need to get back on track.

Key Takeaways

1. No department-wide or company-wide goal is achievable without productive employees.

2. Every employee faces roadblocks to productivity at least some of the time. Three of the most common roadblocks are procrastination, perfectionism, and low self-esteem.

3. Using a time-management matrix can help you and your employees identify the tasks that are most important.

4. Chunking tasks can help eliminate wasted time and boost productivity.

5. Using a timer can help you maintain focus and avoid distractions.

6. An effective leader helps employees identify roadblocks to productivity, and gives employees the tools they need to overcome.

7. Giving feedback is just as important as getting it. When employees know, they will be held accountable on a regular basis, their productivity increases.

11
Using Psychology to Recruit Top Talent

I am convinced that nothing we do is more important than hiring and developing people. At the end of the day you bet on people, not on strategies.
~ Lawrence Bossidy, General Electric

Recruiting top talent is a concern for anybody in a leadership position. Strong leaders understand that a company is only as good as its employees and the relationships between them. Consequently, businesses often spend significant time and effort recruiting and hiring.

Why Recruiting the Right People Is Important

No effective leader would deny that recruiting is essential to the success of their company. No matter how hard you work as a leader, it is not possible to do everything yourself. You must be able to rely upon the people who work for you. This requires taking the time to attract and acquire the right people. Since recruiting is costly, time consuming, and sometimes exhausting, you don't want to waste unnecessary time with the wrong person.

A 2013 CareerBuilder survey showed that more than a quarter of employers (27%) found that a single hiring mistake cost them upwards of $50,000.[1] Keep in mind, that figure represents an average; the cost of hiring the wrong person goes much higher when recruiting high level positions. When you hire the wrong person, the potential exists for that single decision to cost your company millions in lost clients, revenue, and productivity. It's not something that many businesses can afford to take lightly.

Common Hiring Mistakes

Before we talk about some of the ways that you can use psychology to improve your hiring practices, let's talk about some of the mistakes that leaders make when they set out to recruit a new employee. A 2013 Forbes article discussed the importance of recruitment. It outlined how some leaders drop the ball when it comes to hiring.[2]

1. **Rushing the process**. When you lose a valued employee, the temptation will be strong to get a replacement in the door as quickly as possible. The problem with rushing is that you will overlook critical red flags or settle for someone who lacks critical knowledge and abilities. Yes, acting fast for the *right*

applicant is important. However, investing in a high-quality and thorough recruitment process upfront will save you money down the road. Think of the effort and time required not only to get rid of a poor hire, but also to rectify any damage done to the organization.

2. **Prolonging the process**. If rushing the hiring process is a bad idea, drawing it out for longer than necessary is equally harmful. Some leaders find that they feel a sense of paralysis when it comes to making hiring decisions. They don't want to hire someone good in case there's someone perfect who's still out there. The danger with that kind of thinking is that nobody's perfect, so no matter how long you keep looking you are never going to find perfection.

3. **Hiring based on a gut feeling.** Sometimes having a gut feeling about something can be a good thing, but it's not a good idea when it comes to hiring. A skilled interviewee will be able to distract you from things that really matter with a charming manner or flattering statements. It is important to take a step back and really consider each candidate's merits if you want to make the right choice. When making hiring decisions, there are a number of cognitive biases to avoid.

Cognitive Biases That Affect Hiring

As a reminder, cognitive biases are mental glitches—shortcuts that our brains take. They don't always serve us well, and that is certainly true of the biases here.

The Halo Effect and the Horns Effect

The Halo Effect is a cognitive bias that was studied by researchers Nesbitt and Wilson in 1977.[3] It says that our perceptions of people have a significant impact on our evaluation of their skills and qualities. In the study, participants interviewed an instructor. In half of the interviews, the instructor behaved in a warm and friendly manner. In the other half, he was cold and aloof. While his relevant qualities remained unchanged, the study showed that the participants' reactions varied depending on which persona they encountered. The subjects who met the friendly instructor rated him highly, while those who met the aloof instructor were less generous in their assessments. Even though there was sufficient evidence to objectively rate the person's attributes, these ratings were influenced by how friendly the person came across. To cap it off, the subjects were unaware of this bias and they reported that their dislike of the instructor had no effect on their ratings.

An earlier study from 1974 showed that the Halo Effect works in reverse, as well. When it does, it's called the Horns Effect.[4] In this study, readers read an essay supposedly written by a female, college freshman. They then evaluated the quality of the essay and the ability of the writer. By means of a photo attached to the essay, one third of the readers were led to believe that the writer was attractive and one third were led to believe that the writer was unattractive. The other third were given no photo and had no perception of the writer's attractiveness. Half of the essays were also well written and the other half were not. What was found was that readers evaluated the writer and her essay significantly and consistently more favorably when she was attractive. The writer and her essay were evaluated the least favorably when she was unattractive. This effect was found to be the most pronounced for the essays that were objectively of lower quality. Overall, this study showed that the attractiveness of a college student significantly influenced how readers rated their work.

How does this play into your hiring decisions? Mannerisms and physical appearances can directly impact your hiring practices without you even knowing. For example, if you dislike nail biting, an applicant biting their nails once in an interview could result in you rating them less favorably even though biting their nails does not have an effect on how successfully they could perform the job. You can also undervalue some attributes while overvaluing others. A potential employee impressing you in one area can influence your ratings in other areas, without you knowing, and even in the presence of information that clearly indicates that another candidate is preferable.

Leniency/Strictness Bias

The Leniency Bias, and its counterpart the Strictness Bias, can both play a role in hiring decisions. In the leniency bias, an individual is rated more positively than warranted. The strictness bias is the opposite of this. What these biases show is that interviewers can give markedly different evaluations of the same candidate based on their personal biases. For example, an individual panel member can rate more leniently overall or more strictly. In fact, studies have shown that people with conscientious personalities tend to rate more strictly and people with more agreeable personalities tend to rate more leniently.[5]

Equally, panels can rate individuals more leniently or strictly because of particular traits. A 2006 study looked at hiring decisions for people who had physical disabilities and found that the Leniency Effect played a significant role in hiring decisions, with many interviewers rating disabled candidates more leniently than their able-bodied counterparts.[6]

Confirmation Bias

The term Confirmation Bias was first coined by researcher Peter Wason in his 1960 study, *On the failure to eliminate hypotheses in a conceptual task*.[7] In his study, Wason asked participants to identify the rule that governed a sequence of three numbers which he provided. The sequence was 2-4-6. He found that very few of the participants correctly identified the rule. Participants tested hypotheses to *confirm* what they thought was occurring. For example, they tried sequences such as 4-8-10 or 20-22-24. The feedback on these sequences was positive. However, most participants failed to test sequences that might *disprove* their hypothesis. They looked only for information to confirm their hypothesis and stopped investigating. Wason's rule was simply 'increasing numbers' but participants instead came up with very complex and detailed rules to explain the sequence—for example, that the rule was "consecutive even numbers." What this experiment showed was that participants sought out examples and evidence to *confirm* what they already believed to be true. This is the impact of confirmation bias—we have a tendency to search for and favor information that confirms our pre-existing beliefs or hypotheses.

How does this apply to hiring practices? If you review a prospective employee's resume, you may look for information that confirms your expectations. You may look for a particular response in a prospective employee's interview response. Or, if on paper a prospective employee meets your criteria, the questions you ask of their reference could be the ones that confirm what you already believe, and not the questions that could reveal potential red flags.

The Similarity Effect

The Similarity Effect is a cognitive bias that says people are more likely to approve of—and rate highly—those they perceive to be similar to themselves.[8] When an interviewer sees similarities between themselves and a potential employee, the interviewer perceives those similarities as evidence that the person deserves the job.

This is a very easy bias for potential employees to take advantage of. They can do this by doing their research on the hiring committee and finding commonalities. They can then mention these commonalities in interview or in their resume to build a sense of similarity that can work in their favor.

Primacy and Recency Effect

The Primacy Effect is a psychological bias that makes items first presented easier to remember. The recency effect is a psychological bias that makes items most recently presented easier to remember.

When recruiting, this means it will be easier for the panel to recall some of the first and last interviews given and resumes evaluated. This can result in candidates whose resumes or interviews have occurred in the middle of the batch to be overlooked.

Equally, first impressions on a resume or in an interview can impact how the remainder of the resume or interview is rated.

A 1946 study showed the weight people place on first impressions. In the study, participants were given a list of traits that described someone. One half of the group received a list headed by a positive trait, while the rest received a list headed by a negative trait. On the whole, the participants who received the first list rated the person more highly than those who received the second list. [9]

Contrast Effect

The Contrast Effect is a cognitive bias that reflects the tendency to make comparisons. When similar objects are placed near one another, we tend to overestimate their similarity—and we do the same for contrasting objects.[10] A person of average height will appear short next to a tall professional basketball player. In job interviews, an average candidate in a sub-par pool of candidates will look like a star.

Using psychology to minimize cognitive biases in recruitment

The key to minimizing cognitive biases in recruitment is first to be aware of them and make others aware of them, and then to take steps to avoid being influenced by them. All cognitive biases are powerful, but awareness—and a certain knowledge of what to do to counteract them—can help you to minimize their pitfalls.

1. **Educate and make the panel aware of biases.** Make everyone involved in the hiring decision aware of the cognitive biases and their dangers. Instruct them on how best to proceed given their biases and make sure to remind them that your primary criteria are job qualifications and not physical appearance or charm.

2. **Use a diverse selection panel.** Do not allow a selection decision to come down to just one person's judgement. Use a diverse selection panel at all stages of the selection process. Build trust within the group so that the panel members feel comfortable raising concerns when they believe biases might be occurring.

3. **Make a thorough evaluation.** To help weed out candidates who lack experience, thoroughly examine resumes before setting up interviews. This will assist you with the Halo and Horn Effects.

4. **Conduct preliminary telephone interviews.** Narrowing the field further with telephone conversations can mitigate some of the Halo Effect's influence. While its effect still needs to be guarded against, the Halo

Effect is less likely to have a profound effect on the phone than in person.

5. **Conduct structured interviews with clearly defined criteria.** This includes clearly defined and measurable job characteristics, selection criteria, and rating scales. Have standardized interview and referee questions, use weighted selection criteria, and have the panel agree up front which of the criteria is the most important. This will help you minimize a number of cognitive biases, for example the Halo and Horns Effect, in which panel members may rate some characteristics more strongly than others. When interviewers must adhere to objective standards when rating interviewees, they are less likely to allow personal biases to get in the way.

6. **Ask follow-up questions.** During interviews, ask follow-up questions, and don't assume you know the answer. Learn how to be quiet and let the prospect answer the question fully.

7. **Use a note taker.** Have someone in the room whose purpose is to record the interviews. This will allow you to look back at the *evidence* that was provided in the interview.

8. **Rate candidates based on evidence.** Use evidence to rate candidates, and compare that evidence against the selection criteria. Do not go by instinct.

9. **Rate independently first before moderating scores.** One panel member can influence others with their biases. For this reason, have panel members rate candidates independently against the evidence before bringing everyone together to moderate scores.

10. **Consider the reliability of your raters.** This can help you to reduce leniency and strictness bias. You can use your HR team or an external program to examine rating trends to determine if biases might be occurring. Look out for instances where a panel member might be consistently more favorable or harsh in rating an applicant.

11. **Recruit for characteristics that are difficult to train.** In the recruitment process, look for skills, abilities, and traits that are difficult to train but important to the job. Difficult to train traits include motivation, passion, resilience, ability to learn quickly, leadership ability, and compatibility with culture. Technical knowledge is often much easier to learn than critical, softer skills. This also relates to promotions—do not promote people to management positions just because of their technical ability.

12. **Check references.** It is very easy for candidates to use cognitive biases against you. Dishonesty in resumes and interviews is also very common. For these

reasons, reference checking is very important. Equally important is the introduction of the "threat" of reference checking at every stage of the process, starting with the job advertisement. Tell candidates that you will be checking information that they supply in their resume and interview with their previous managers. This will encourage greater honesty from the start.

13. **Attract top talent.** You will be in a better position if you are assessing a pool full of high-potential candidates rather than a pool of second or third tier players. Attracting the best candidates to the job comes down to the job advertisement and getting the advertisement out to your network.

    In the advertisement, you should present a realistic job preview so that the successful candidate knows exactly what they are getting into—thus increasing the likelihood that they will stay. The last thing that you want is to go through the costly and time-consuming process of recruiting, only to have the successful candidate leave within the first few months because of mismatched expectations. Just in case, use an order of merit to help speed up the process if the successful person does leave or does not accept the position.

    Sell the benefits of the role. If the salary is favorable, list it to attract high calibre people.

Think carefully about the job title you use to advertise the role. People will make a decision to look at the role purely on the job title. You do not want a title so complex that high-calibre applicants are unsure what exactly the role entails. Job hunting takes time and you need to make it easy for the right applicants. Likewise, if you are trying to attract high-calibre staff for a high-level role, the title you use can make all the difference. Is the title of the job one that will help them build credibility? Is the title equal to or a step up from their current title? Is the title one that they would be proud to tell others? For example, tilting a role 'Manager of ...' versus 'Director or Head of ...' can make a difference.

14. **Don't make the selection process too easy.** A selection process where applicants need to jump through a few hoops is not necessarily a bad thing. This discourages people who are looking for any job, helping to weed them out of the process or keeping them from applying in the first place. The more time and effort that applicants put into the process, the more likely they are going to be thankful for the opportunity and want to stick around. However, this is a fine balance; you also do not want to drag out the process with unnecessary steps and risk losing high-calibre applicants.

Key Takeaways

1. Successful leaders understand that they cannot be successful without hiring the right employees, and that hiring mistakes can be costly.

2. Common hiring mistakes include rushing the process, prolonging the process, or making decisions based on a gut feeling instead of evidence.

3. The Halo Effect and its counterpart, the Horns Effect, can lead interviewers to overrate or underrate interviewees' skills and qualifications based on external qualities such as physical appearance, likeability, and charm.

4. The Confirmation Bias can cause interviewers to skip crucial questions in favor of those that confirm what they already believe to be true.

5. The Similarity Effect can lead interviewers to overrate interviewees who remind them of themselves.

6. The Primacy Effect shows that first impressions can have a lot to do with hiring decisions.

7. The Contrast Effect can lead companies to hire the best of a sub-par group of candidates.

8. The key to overcoming cognitive biases is to strategically target them through structured and consistent processes that increase objectivity.

12
Using Psychology to Enhance Feedback

I think it's very important to have a feedback loop, where you're constantly thinking about what you've done and how you could do it better.

~ Elon Musk

No matter how skilled an employee is, there will be times when, for whatever reason, they are not meeting your expectations. And even good employees who are doing well have things they can improve on, and need to hear how they're doing. Learning to give constructive feedback will allow employees to improve their performance.

What Is Feedback?

Many leaders make the mistake of incorrectly defining feedback. There is a tendency to think of feedback as an opportunity to let employees know your opinion of their work, but when defined too narrowly, feedback can fall on deaf ears.

In broad terms, feedback is "information regarding the gap between an input level (employee job performance) and a reference level (a job description and/or your expectations) of a system parameter."[1] The parameter is defined in any way you choose, including:

1. Output (the employee's production and results)
2. Input (the employee's time and effort)
3. Process (the employee's methods)

To provide your employees with effective feedback, you must have all three things: parameters, input levels, and actual levels. The absence of any one will render the feedback ineffective. In other words, you cannot provide effective feedback without having measured the employee's work in some quantifiable or qualitative way, and making clear what your expectations are.

It is also important to note that employees in different areas of the world will vary in their desire for feedback.[2] Employers with a diverse or multinational workforce must take cultural differences into consideration. For instance, when seeking feedback, employees from Asian descent tend to be less forthright in sharing their views on anything negative. They tend to be less inclined to talk badly of their superiors. They also tend to be less likely to say if a deadline is not achievable, and need to be encouraged and given permission to ask for more time where reasonable.

Types of Feedback

Feedback in the workplace can take several forms. The appropriateness of the type of feedback will depend on the situation.[3] There are four basic types of feedback:

1. **Positive reinforcement** is feedback that is meant to boost morale. It is useful at times of high stress when employees have taken on challenges or put in extra time at work.

2. **Evaluative feedback** usually takes the form of a performance review and involves a comparison of employee performance to a job description or list of expectations.

3. **Warnings** are typically given when an employee's performance is faltering. Warnings can be oral or written, but their aim is to allow employees a chance to correct their course and improve their performance.

4. **Admonishments** should be rare and issued only when an employee has done something wrong. For example, if you notice that an employee is using the internet for personal business or taking extra-long lunch breaks, you will need to give them an admonishment.

Feedback can be delivered one-on-one or in group feedback. Group feedback should take the form of positive reinforcement or evaluative feedback, since warnings and admonishments should be delivered in private—unless they involve the entire group.

Another highly effective type of feedback is 360 degree feedback. You have probably been exposed to this before.[4] This is feedback that comes not only from leaders but from all the people around an employee: direct reports, peers, clients, vendors, and management. Many of the top companies in the world have widely implemented 360 degree feedback as a way of getting a complete picture of job performance. Instead of using a single parameter, such as employee output, it takes multiple parameters into consideration.

Becoming more common is 540 degree feedback, in which feedback from an employee's boss' boss is also included. This system of feedback can be particularly effective with high-potential employees who at some stage are likely to be promoted and so the employee can better understand how they are perceived at a higher level.

720 degree feedback by far is the most effective and recent feedback system and involves undertaking 360 or 540 degree feedback at least twice, at two different points in time; most commonly 12 months apart. This allows the employee and the organization to get a baseline of performance, create

an enhancement or improvement plan, and after 12 months check the level of improvement that may or may not have occurred.

Why Feedback Is Important

Giving regular feedback to employees is essential. An Israeli study that trained managers in effective feedback techniques found that employees who received constructive feedback did a better job than those who did not.[5] It also found that combining feedback with goal setting was especially effective and resulted in stronger employee performance.

The lesson we can take from this is that delivering regular, constructive feedback to your staff should be mandatory, not optional. Your employees need guidance and you and your leadership group are in the best position to give it to them. A note of caution is appropriate, however, because poorly delivered feedback can be extremely damaging, as can no feedback at all. How do you avoid this? By training your leadership group, at a minimum, in the psychology of feedback, and modeling a culture of feedback in your organization.

Case Study – Feedback

Let's look at an example from my experience to see how misunderstood feedback can cause a problem. (Note the client job role has been changed to protect client confidentiality). A public defender gets feedback from her boss, who tells her that she needs to be less personally involved in her cases. He doesn't elaborate, and she dismisses what he tells her as wrong. She believes that he's telling her to be less passionate about what she does, or to spend less time forming a personal connection with the people she represents.

However, what her boss is really concerned about is that she has no boundaries with her clients. He worries that she is crossing lines that shouldn't be crossed and wants to make sure that she understands that her behavior is affecting her clients and the public defender's office.

The issue here is two-sided. She doesn't ask for clarification—instead, she jumps to a conclusion about what her boss means. And he doesn't offer specifics, leaving his words open to interpretation.

As a leader, you must make certain that your subordinates know what your feedback means, and give concrete examples, if you expect it to be received well. A boss who was highly skilled at offering feedback would let the employee know what the problems were—as well as why they were a problem—rather than offering non-specific feedback that left open the possibility of misinterpretation.

Psychological Principles to Delivering Effective Feedback

The idea of delivering feedback to employees can be intimidating, particularly to leaders who haven't received formal training in how to do so. However, there are some psychological principles that you can use to help you deliver meaningful and effective feedback that will help your employees and you grow.

1. **Forget about the so-called feedback sandwich**. The feedback sandwich is a theory, still popular in certain circles, that says that employees will be better able to accept criticism of their performance if you "sandwich" it between positive comments.[6] However, there is evidence to suggest that is not the case, and that the improvement comment will actually end up getting lost in the process if you use the feedback sandwich. With the feedback-sandwich approach, too much time is spent building up the employee to buffer them against the negative comment to come, and then letting the employee down gently with what is often a forced positive comment. The negative comment is like a piece of ham that has been sliced too thinly and put on a cheap sandwich with thick bread—you can find it if you look for it, but it won't be what you remember about the sandwich.

Effective delivery of improvement feedback should not require a buffer. It should flow in the conversation and help employees better understand their current performance and the desired changes that you hope to elicit from them. The trust and positive relationship that you have with the person receiving the feedback should be the buffer to help them through the process, not the forced positive comments to either side of the improvement comment.

2. **Positive comments.** It is fine and effective to mention positive comments when delivering feedback. Just so they are not forced and are there to do more than buffer the upcoming improvement comment. Also, make sure that the positive comments relate to the improvement comment. For example, do not say, "You look nice today. I really need you to keep me informed more often." Instead a related and genuine positive comment could be, "You are really stepping up and taking on more responsibility and, to help you further, I need you to keep me informed more often...."

3. **Don't use the word 'but'.** The word "but" tends to incite a particular reaction in people who hear it. It undercuts anything positive you have just said and can put people on the defensive.[7] Instead of saying, "You do a great job but..." say, "You do a great job AND you could do

even better if you...." This change from "but" to "and" makes a big difference in how employees will receive the feedback you give them. Rather than ignoring anything before the "but," they will be more receptive to both the positive and improvement comments.

4. **Because.** One study looked at the power of justification when asking someone to make an adjustment in their behavior. In the study, people waiting in line to use a copy machine were asked to let someone cut in.[8] In the absence of any explanation, the answer was usually, "No." However, when the person asking offered an explanation, such as, "Can I cut in because I'm in a rush?" or "Can I cut in because I only have a few copies?" the other people waiting were significantly more likely to agree. The most interesting finding from this study was the key differentiator was the word "because." Irrespective of the reason given, people were more likely to let the person cut in the line if they used the word "because" followed by some kind of reason.

The key takeaway here is, when delivering feedback, use the word "because" immediately after the improvement comment and provide a reason behind why you are asking for this improvement. So, rather than saying, "You need to keep me informed more often," you would say, "You need to keep me informed more often *because* this will allow me to provide you with extra information you may not have, and allow me to help you when needed."

5. **Feedback structure**. Let's combine what has been covered so far. Rather than using the feedback sandwich, the structure of your feedback should instead look like:

[Positive comment that relates to your improvement comment] AND [improvement comment] BECAUSE [reason behind the improvement comment].

What these psychological principles demonstrate is that the form in which you present feedback is just as important as the content of your feedback.

Lessons for Leaders

Now that you understand some of the psychological principles behind structuring effective feedback, let's look at some psychological research and tools to help you to further enhance your feedback approach.

1. **Determine the appropriate setting in which to provide feedback**. At times, it will be appropriate to give team feedback. Other times, however, individual feedback is more effective.[9] Give team feedback

when more than one person on the team is affected by an aspect of performance, or when the feedback comes from team members. You should also give team feedback when an issue arises that affects most of the team. Individual feedback is best when an issue does not affect other team members. Individual feedback is also often needed after delivering team feedback to support your message and ensure that all members have understood it clearly.

2. **Keep experience levels in mind when delivering feedback.** Tailor the tone of your feedback to employees' experience levels. A 2012 study found that beginners who received positive feedback were likely to feel encouraged and committed to continuing their efforts.[10] However, upper-level employees who received positive feedback took it as a sign that their efforts had been only sufficient and were likely to perform badly as a result. The reverse was true with negative feedback.

Keep experience levels in mind when you are giving out feedback. Remember that high-level employees are more receptive to targeted improvement feedback that focuses on what they need to do to improve, and that entry-level employees are likely to be more receptive to positive feedback.

3. **Be specific.** It's not enough to speak in generalizations. We all have a tendency to make assumptions. We take mental shortcuts and read incorrect meanings into things. The only way to be sure that your employees are going to be able to respond appropriately to the feedback you give them is to be as specific and concrete as possible. That way, you're providing employees with a clear roadmap for success.

4. **Check understanding.** Another technique that works well is to encourage your employees to repeat your feedback in their own words. Even effective communicators can fall into the trap of using convenient labels when providing feedback.[11] If feedback is misinterpreted by your employees and you provide it in a way that doesn't allow them an opportunity to ask questions, you run the risk that they will make the wrong changes. Make sure that they understand your points before you discuss expectations and what they can do to improve their performance.

5. **Provide *regular* feedback.** It's not enough to give feedback once and then assume that employees will do what they need to do. Rather, feedback should be ongoing.[12] When you provide feedback, whether it's in the form of a performance review or an admonishment, set up a regular schedule to follow up. It is helpful to

set short-term and long-term goals so that you have additional parameters to use to evaluate employees' progress. The key is not to wait. Follow up as often as you need to so your employees always know where they stand.

6. **Use 720, 540 or 360 degree feedback.** Tailoring who gives feedback to whom, and when, is an effective aid in achieving organizational goals and building a stronger corporate culture. Evidence suggests that this type of feedback is most effective when it is tailored to a specific goal or set of goals. For example, Standard & Poor's used 360 degree feedback to build a company culture that makes performance its top priority.[13] They include a self-assessment, an assessment by a manager, and three additional assessments that come from co-workers, clients, or other people in the employee's sphere. They have been using 360 degree feedback for more than 20 years.

The bottom line is that the feedback you give to employees is only going to be successful if you deliver it in a way that is constructive and specific, and sets them up for success. If you heed the psychological principles in this chapter when providing feedback, your employees will be able to learn, grow, and improve.

Key Takeaways

1. To give effective feedback, you must have a reference level, an input level, and a measurable parameter.

2. Employee performance can be measured based on input (employee effort), output (employee production), or process (employee methods.)

3. Creating a dialogue with feedback is more effective than masking criticism with positive feedback.

4. Give employees reasons for your improvement feedback to attach meaning to what they need to do to improve.

5. Give more effective feedback by using the word "and" instead of the word "but."

6. Give feedback in an appropriate setting—provide group feedback only when issues affect the entire group. Otherwise, feedback should be provided in a one-on-one setting.

7. Remember that entry-level employees respond best to positive feedback while high-level employees respond best to improvement feedback.

8. Be very specific when providing feedback, and have employees repeat feedback to ensure that they understand.

9. Follow up regularly after providing feedback to ensure that your employees are making progress and meeting short-term goals.

10. Consider implementing 360 degree feedback widely across your organization to get a clear picture of every aspect of performance.

13
Using Psychology to Handle Conflict and Deal with Difficult People

Conflict can and should be handled constructively; when it is, relationships benefit. Conflict avoidance is not the hallmark of a good relationship. On the contrary, it is a symptom of serious problems and of poor communication.

~ Harriet B. Braiker

As much as most people dislike conflict, it is both impossible and unwise to avoid it. In any situation where more than one person is working, it is inevitable that they will have differences of opinion. Every individual has unique life experiences that have brought them to where they are, and those experiences often produce strikingly different viewpoints about how things are or should be.

The key to dealing with conflict is to understand its psychology and to resolve it in constructive ways.

What Is Conflict Resolution?

Simply put, conflict is any situation in which desires, facts, or fears pull people in divergent directions.[1] Note that a conflict does not have to be a fight. As long as there is a difference in terms of feelings or goals, there is conflict. Conflict resolution, then, is the process used to get the people involved in the conflict to an area of common ground—or, if that isn't possible, to defuse the anger and create a stable environment in which people can work with one another.

Managing conflict in the workplace can be both time-consuming and expensive. In recent years, the number of employees in the United States who said they were willing to consider suing for employer discrimination rose to 62%.[2] Litigation is often seen as a conflict resolution tool, but it is important for leaders to work at resolving conflict before it reaches a courtroom.

Some of the most common conflicts that arise in the workplace include:

- Accusations of employer discrimination or favoritism
- Complaints from customers about employees
- Disagreements between employees, including interpersonal conflict
- Disagreements between leaders and employees

Each conflict that arises is unique, and yet they all still share some basic components. The key to being able to use conflict resolution successfully as a leader is to understand the nature of conflict in general, and then to use strategies to help the participants negotiate a way out of their—or even your—disagreement.

Case Study

Politics offers us many high-stakes examples of leaders and how they react to conflict. Let's look at two from American history, both of which are illustrative of how conflict can be resolved—and even be helpful.

1. President Abraham Lincoln knew that he couldn't surround himself with yes-men if he wanted to lead his country through turbulent times. He chose to appoint a cabinet filled with people who had divergent and sometimes opposing opinions.[3] Sometimes referred to as his "Team of Rivals," these people helped Lincoln lead the United States through its most profound conflict, the American Civil War.

2. In 1977, President Jimmy Carter took office with the idea that he wanted to do something to bring about peace in the Middle East. He and his team of diplomats worked tirelessly for over 14 months to broker a peace agreement between Egypt and Israel. They hoped

to find a resolution to the Israeli-Palestinian conflict.[4] The negotiations ended with the famous Camp David Accords, that led to the hoped-for deal between Israeli leader Menachem Begin and Egyptian leader Anwar Sadat.

What these two examples show is that conflict is necessary at times, particularly in situations where it is important to hear a variety of opinions. They also show that it is possible to resolve even the thorniest conflict through diligent effort.

Psychological Principles of Conflict Resolution

Telling people to stop or getting angry with them won't end conflict, and is likely to instead exacerbate it. Understanding the psychology behind diffusing conflict can better equip you to deal with conflict as it arises. Here are some of the key principles and tools of conflict resolution—tools that you can use to intervene before conflict escalates to a place that requires external intervention.

1. **The Harvard Approach** to conflict resolution draws a distinction between participants' positions (*what* they say they want) and their interests (*why* they say they want it).[5] According to the model, the way to resolve conflict is to get parties to focus on their interests, with the idea that there is more common ground to be found

there than in their opposing positions. For example, two people could have a common interest in attracting new clients, but differing opinions about how to do it. When managing conflict, ask, "So, what are you really interested in?" Then ask, "Why do you want this?" When asking this, you want to focus on factors that identify the underlying foundation for their positions. These include desires and concerns. Focusing on interests is valuable because it increases collaboration, can open up more options for the parties involved, and makes it easier to find solutions. In fact, parties often find through this process that they have shared interests.

The Harvard Approach is equally important for you as a leader as well—consider your interests when managing a conflict.

2. **Needs theory** is another principle that helps leaders to develop an understanding of the roots of conflict. It says that most people fall into one of three "needs" categories: achievement (the need to feel they have accomplished something), affiliation (the need to feel a sense of belonging and acceptance), or power (the need for personal prestige and status).[6] When you understand which needs are most important to the parties in a conflict, you will be better able to come up with a resolution that will work for all.

3. **The theory of conflict transformation** argues that conflict resolution requires more than just the identification of win-win outcomes. Conflict transformation is instead a process of engaging with and transforming the relationships, interests, and discourses of parties. It requires the person trying to resolve the conflict to develop a deep understanding of the participants' motives and feelings.[7] Once the negotiator can empathize with all parties, their job is to first introduce compassion and creativity to the proceedings. Then, they encourage parties to arrive at a solution that will allow them to resolve it.[8]

   Note: Conflict transformation is a gradual process achieved through a series of smaller and larger changes. Not all parties are likely to move at the same pace.

4. **The Betari Box** is a model that can help leaders identify the root causes of conflict. It links behavior and attitude. The Betari Box helps parties to understand the impact that attitudes and behaviors have on others. For example, when we are feeling motivated and positive we smile, compliment others, and are more inclined to do favors for people. The opposite is true when we are feeling negatively, and can be impatient or angry.

The Betari Box shows that all conflict is cyclical.[9] For example, party A's attitude affects their behavior. Their behavior in turn affects the attitude of party B. Party B's attitude affects their behavior, which then affects party A's attitude… and so on. Once all parties realize that their attitude and behavior is impacting the conflict—and that their behavior is something they can control—they are better positioned to rein it in and stop the cycle. Use the Betari Box to show parties the cycle of behavior and attitude, that our behaviors and attitudes contribute to the cycle, and that we all have a choice in how we can respond to situations. For leaders, it is also important to address unacceptable attitudes to minimize this cycle of behavior.

5. **Conflict mapping** gives a bird's eye view of the conflict. It is a way of graphically representing the conflict, showing everyone's perspectives and helping to move toward solutions that will meet as many parties' needs as possible. Conflict mapping can be used with individuals or groups and encourages parties to consider the issue from the other party's perspective. It can be used for simple or complex issues.[10]

The first step in using conflict mapping involves defining the issue. This should be done by the parties involved. The issue should not identify a person as the problem.

Instead the issue should be labeled in broad objective terms and in a way that all parties to the conflict agree. For example, rather than "X person is lazy," the issue would be "workload division." Once the issue is agreed, write this in a circle in the middle of the page/whiteboard/screen.

The next step is to identify all of the major parties. This could be individuals, teams, or groups. Include people who may affect or be involved in the conflict both directly and indirectly. Help the individual/group write a list first and then, once the parties agree, place the names of the major parties on the page/whiteboard/screen, equally spaced around the issue. Draw lines to separate each party around the identified issue.

Next, list the major needs and concerns of each party. Look for both tangible needs (such as more space, a tidy place to work) and intangible needs (such as a feeling of security, acknowledgement). If conflict mapping is being done as a group, ask each party to share their needs and concerns related to the issue. If conflict mapping is being done with an individual, ask them to think about what the needs and concerns of each party might be. This encourages individuals to put themselves in the "other party's shoes." Write these needs and concerns on the conflict map.

What you end up with is a visual representation of the issue and all parties' needs and concerns. This helps parties to identify common ground. The process itself can help parties to find new perspectives and ways of thinking about the issue. Using the process to ask "why" and uncover greater depth to people's expressed needs will help the parties come to a solution.

6. **Joint problem-solving** is the best method of conflict resolution in situations in which there is a conflict between people who must work closely with one another.[11] In a situation where strong conflict exists, parties are less willing to accept solutions they had no part in developing. Therefore, both parties must be willing to work together to arrive at a mutually agreeable solution. The ability to do so is a key indicator of success in partnerships. If you find that parties are unable to come up with a joint solution, you can assist with presenting the parties with three options. You have defined the options based on what you have heard. However, you are encouraging their ownership by having them choose the option that they agree to try.

The key to each of these principles is being as analytical and objective as possible rather than getting caught up in your own perspective as a leader—or the perspective of one party.

These principles also help you to look at the big picture and encourage parties to own solutions.

Applications for Your Organization

Now it's time to consider some additional practical approaches that you can use in your organization to better manage conflict. Employees won't always be able to see their way out of a conflict, but you can help them do so.

1. **Be aware**. The first thing you must do is be aware of conflicts when they arise. If people in your department or organization are having a problem, you must ensure that you will find out about it as quickly as possible. This does not mean that you need to get involved. Instead, use your organization's governance and processes for dealing with conflict and employee issues. Make sure that problems are not being escalated. Instead observe, coach your leaders on managing the conflict appropriately, and intervene when necessary. Sometimes, parties in conflict can be very skilled at hiding their disagreements. Be aware of the fallout associated with conflict as it will help point you in the direction of the conflict itself.

2. **Use reflective listening.** To get at the heart of a conflict, reflective listening can work well. Reflective listening is listening that requires you to understand

the participants' feelings and mirror them back.[12] For example, if you listened to an employee and realized that they were feeling undermined by a co-worker, you might say to them, "It sounds as though you feel your authority is being undermined." Make sure that you truly listen and read the situation accurately. If you do, such statements can make the employee feel understood and help you with the resolution process.

3. **Timing.** When managing conflict, give parties time to compose themselves and think about the issue at hand. Springing a conflict resolution meeting on an employee can backfire. Instead, if employees have time to think about the matter beforehand, it can do a great deal to lay the groundwork for a successful meeting. You can even discuss the matter one-on-one first and talk to them about tools such as the Betari Box to help them think through the problem. Give parties time to think about their own attitudes and behavior.

4. **Evaluate the parties' primary needs.** Remember the three primary needs: achievement, affiliation, and power. Ask yourself if they are responsible for the conflict. For example, two employees who both feel a strong need for power are likely to end up in conflict with one another. As a leader, you can find ways to

make them both feel empowered, thus resolving the conflict.

5. **Know your boundaries.** Each person deals with conflict differently. Know the boundaries and triggers of parties involved as well as your own. Consider when to take a break, when to push, and when not to.

6. **Respect differences.** Conflict resolution is never black and white. The workplace is becoming more culturally and generationally diverse. People are driven by different values and points of view. As a leader, do what you can to show that you are impartial to the process. Go in as an empty bucket and give all parties the opportunity to be heard and not judged.

7. **Call out the elephant in the room**. Confront the underlying issue rather than skirting over it and allowing it to fester.

All of the above techniques are practical and can be used in a variety of situations. Conflict happens, whether we want it to or not. It is natural because people are different. We have different ideas, different values, different viewpoints, and experience emotions and cognitive biases. Conflict can be beneficial because it can expose problems you were otherwise unaware of, allowing you to eliminate them. Just be sure to work to eliminate them effectively.

Key Takeaways

1. Conflict is defined as a situation wherein participants' desires, needs, or fears pull them in divergent directions.

2. Conflict is unavoidable, and often necessary, to the success of an organization or endeavor.

3. Avoiding conflict can be detrimental in a variety of ways, both financially and emotionally.

4. Effective conflict resolution starts with helping parties to find common ground in terms of their shared interests.

5. Most people feel a strong need for achievement, affiliation, or power. Understanding their needs can lead to compassion and empathy, both of which can help resolve conflicts.

6. Looking at a conflict in a big-picture way, and helping participants to see how their own attitudes and behaviors affect each other, is a good way to work toward conflict resolution.

7. Joint problem solving is often the best way to get two warring parties to a place where they agree with one another.

8. As a leader, reflective listening will help you get to the heart of a conflict so you can help the participants work through it.

Key Takeaways

14
The Psychology of Teams

Great things in business are never done by one person. They're done by a team of people.
~ Steve Jobs

Just as a strong chain is made of strong links, strong companies are made of strong teams, and great leaders are always backed by great teams.

What Is a Team?

Teams are not just any group of people. A team is a group of people who work toward a shared goal in an efficient and harmonious manner.[1] Referring to a divided and inharmonious group as a team would be inaccurate. For a group of people to form a team, every person must make a diligent effort to meet the shared goal, and each person should be assigned work that aligns with their strengths and capabilities. While conflict and differences of opinions are inevitable in most teams, most teams only win after they learn to work together in harmony.

For example, imagine a scenario in which a leader assembles a group of employees and asks them to revamp the company's Customer Resource Management (CRM) system. The leader makes no effort to get the employees on the same page, and the employees are not encouraged to work together. As a result, each employee has their own ideas about how the CRM system should work and sets about to make those changes. Instead of working together to come up with a clear, practical solution, the group's members are at odds with one another. Petty squabbles and infighting are inevitable, and the CRM system will remain ineffective.

If, instead, the leader had given the group a framework for their task and found ways to turn them into a fully functioning team, the result would be very different. Instead of working against one another and wasting time over unnecessary issues, they would be more inclined to work together, with each member of the team contributing what they could toward a common goal.

Why Are Teams and Effective Teamwork So Important?

There are many reasons that teamwork is important, one of which is that teamwork and performance are directly linked. When people are working at cross-purposes to one another, the dissonance has an impact on results. Here are some specific effects of teamwork.

- A 2003 study showed that engineering teams working on software development were far more likely to arrive at groundbreaking and exciting solutions when they worked efficiently as a team.[2]

- A 2002 study of medical teams revealed that teamwork training had a huge impact on patient results. In fact, the rate of errors in the experimental group was reduced from 30.9% before the training to only 4.4% after the training.[3]

- Organizations that use self-directed teams of workers to accomplish tasks are found to be 30% more productive than organizations that don't use teams.[4]

- Research suggests that one of the biggest benefits of teamwork is that, when teams are properly assembled and represent a variety of backgrounds, opinions, and skills, the resultant team performs at a higher cognitive level than any individual or homogeneous team would.[5]

As you can see, encouraging effective teamwork can have a positive effect for organizations.

Case Study: Google

Few people would argue against considering Google as one of the most innovative and successful companies in the world today. To understand the roots of Google's success, we can look at its origins. The original concept was the brainchild of a small team of two: Larry Page and Sergey Brin, the founders of the company. They worked through the technology together, each man bringing his own strengths and ideas to bear on their shared goal.[6]

They expanded the team only when they were ready to launch the company and found that they needed other viewpoints and expertise. At that point, they brought in two additional team members: Eric Schmidt to run the company and handle the business side of things, and Omar Kordestani to manage sales.

Note that each team member contributed something different to the goal of launching the company. Page and Brin shared a goal but realized they needed additional team members to help them achieve it.

The key lessons from this example are that each person on the team brought something important to the table. The team was also only as large as it needed to be at the time. The number of people on the team was less important than the sum total of their capabilities and skills. And all team members understood the common goals for the team. Each of these elements is important for building effective teams.

Psychological Principles for Building Strong Teams

There are a number of key researched, tried, and tested principles that contribute to building effective teams. These include:

1. **Group identity**. One of the keys to building functional teams is to ensure that teams have a strong group identity. A 1997 study found that teams with a strong sense of cohesion and identity were more productive, and had a greater positive impact on the organization, than teams that had only a weak identity.[7]

    As a team leader, you can help teams create an identity. You cannot force group identity but you can guide it. You can do this by:

    a. Working with the group to identify who they are, what drives them as a group, what they are trying to achieve, what is important to them as individuals, and if there are sets of agreed attitudes, customs, and expectations.

    b. Setting the vision and the direction for the group, and guiding agreement on the team goals. Group members will feel solidarity with each other when they perceive that they are working toward shared ends. Write down these goals and the mission for the group and reinforce them regularly.

c. Clarifying the expected attitudes that should guide the team. You should both guide these expectations and invite the group to take ownership of their own expectations for their fellow group members. Ask the team what they need and expect from you as their leader.

d. Making connections in the group and finding commonalities. People feel connected to others when there are perceived commonalities. Provide ways for group members to have shared experiences. For example, team-building exercises, birthday celebrations, and leadership retreats. Encourage members to discuss these experiences and to use them in their work.

e. Emphasizing the importance of roles and ensuring that they do not overlap or that you do not have a group of people all doing similar things. To assist with role identification, help group members identify and share their strengths, experience, and what motivates them. When people feel that they play an important role in the group, they will have a sense of solidarity with other group members.

All of these actions will help you to inform group identity leading to a more united, positive, and productive group of leaders.

2. **Company culture.** The trust that employees have in the organization correlates highly to their level of teamwork. A 2003 study found that employees who believed in the company were better team players than those who were merely working for a paycheck.[8] The study also found that trustworthiness and perceived progress were significant factors in team effectiveness. Finding ways to improve corporate culture and increase employees' commitment to the company on an emotional level will have a positive effect on teamwork, productivity, and performance.

Have you given team members a reason to believe in the organization? If you don't have a clearly defined corporate culture, now is the time to start building one. Link the goals of the team to your organizational goals, and make sure that those goals are something that people can invest in emotionally. It is also helpful to set up some metrics to measure the team's progress. Perceived progress can go a long way in cementing team trust and the desired company culture.

3. **Diversity.** In teams, diversity matters. Diverse cities experience more economic growth, and companies

with at least one female board member outperform those with no female representation. Diversity brings many benefits *provided that the workplace is harmonious*. Research shows that well-managed, diverse teams outperform homogeneous teams. However, when diverse teams are not managed well, trust and communication can dissolve, resulting in lower performance. Diversity relies on social cohesion (unity and trust). Social cohesion involves managing compliance factors such as harassment, equal opportunity, and equity; organizational factors such as knowledge and people management; and market factors such as industrial and community relations. Focus on these foundational factors first, and then encourage diversity in practices such recruitment and training.

4. **Personality types**. As with other forms of diversity, different personalities bring different strengths to the table, and a functional team needs many of them to succeed. In fact, a 1997 study found that the success of a team was directly linked to having a good balance of personality types.[9] In other words, when a team is improperly balanced, it will not function at a high level. For your teams, look at the personality profiles of group members and identify gaps to be filled. The Team Management Systems Worldwide (TMS) platform is just

one tool that can assist you with this. The TMS platform maps work and personality preferences to eight work functions that are critical for any fully functioning team. As noted above, diversity works when there is good management. Having people with different personalities in teams can bring the risk of personality clashes. But when there is strong management, agreed upon team rules, respect, trust, and appreciation for diversity, this risk is mitigated.

5. **Social skills.** When you are putting together a team for a project, what do you prioritize? Intelligence and know-how, or social skills? A 2010 study found that social skills were a far stronger predictor of group success than the average intelligence of group members.[10] It also found that there was a direct correlation between the number of women on a team and the team's success—specifically, that groups with a higher percentage of gender diversity tended to have better social skills, and therefore higher collective intelligence, than those with a low percentage of women.

6. **Humor.** Humor plays an important role in teamwork. For example, a 2007 study found that the judicious use of humor in the workplace, particularly in teams, can act as a social lubricant and help increase feelings of solidarity.[11] It also found that humor is an effective way

of softening criticism or negative feedback. The key is to be careful that one team member doesn't end up bearing the brunt of the humor and feeling ostracized from teammates.

7. **Team dysfunction.** Team dysfunction is usually the result of one (or more) of five problems. They include a lack of trust, fear of conflict, lack of commitment, avoidance of accountability, and inattention to results.[7] When one member of a team demonstrates any one of these dysfunctions, it can impact the performance of the entire team. If you want your team to be a success, you must root out each one of these dysfunctions and address it directly.

There are many factors that influence an effective, high-performing team. The above factors are all researched, tried and tested, and have been proven to provide a strong foundation for building successful teams.

Applications for Your Organization

As you can see, there is more to team building than simply grouping employees based on their work-related capabilities. Keeping in mind the psychology of team building, here are some additional practical tools to assist you:

1. **Team-building activities**. Even a team that's been carefully constructed based on social skills and personality types can benefit from team-building activities. A team-building activity can be as simple as a regular group outing, a series of trust-building exercises, or even a weekend at a team-building retreat. But don't just run a team building activity for the sake of it. Make the wrong choice on the type of team-building activity and instead it can be an expensive "learning opportunity."

   The purpose of team building activities is to be an educational tool to *facilitate* those difficult conversations and "aha" moments. It is not about the activity itself, it is about the facilitation and debrief of the activity.

   Before deciding on a team-building activity, there are many things to consider. What is the end goal? What change in behaviors are you looking for? Will a team-building activity assist with this? How do you know that the activity is a success? What does success look like? What activity will help you to achieve what you want? Will all team members be willing to participate? Is the activity within budget? Is there any physical or psychological risk? Have you chosen the right person to facilitate the process? What is the follow-up plan to cement lessons learned, after the activity, once everyone returns back to the job? What is the plan for evaluating the success and positive impact of the activity immediately, 3-months later, and 6-months later?

2. **Clearly defining each team member's role.** When job responsibilities and roles are left undefined, it can lead to infighting and distrust. Imagine if every time a baseball team took the field, players were bickering about who would play first base. It's simply not possible for a team to operate well if the players don't know what they're supposed to be doing. Team members need to understand who is responsible for what. You do not need to define every task. Instead focus on lines of responsibility. This works just like Apples' "directly responsible individuals" (DRI) approach. With the DRI approach there is no question about ownership and you do not have 15 people all worrying about the same issue.

3. **Creating a shared goal.** A 2010 study that looked at trauma teams in a medical center found that the teams who shared a mental model—a vision of the group's collective goal—were far more efficient and successful than teams that lacked such a model.[12] You have the power to provide the teams that report to you with clear goals, and the benefits of doing so are significant. To be

effective, a goal cannot be nebulous. The goal should be measurable and achievable, and all team members should have a full understanding of what the goal is and how you expect them to reach it.

4. **Observation.** Finally, keep an eye out for signs of any team dysfunction and make sure to nip it in the bud. One misunderstanding or underperforming member can sink the entire team effort, so don't make the mistake of assuming that things will work themselves out. Confront problems head-on, give team feedback where appropriate, and re-assign team members as needed.

Use these techniques to ensure that the teams in your organization are successful. Keep in mind, too, that many of the psychological principles that apply to small teams apply to your organization as a whole. Shared vision and goals, personality balance, and trust are important to the success of any organization.

Key Takeaways

1. A team is a group of people who work together toward a shared goal in a harmonious and efficient manner.
2. Strong teamwork is essential if you want to create an environment where innovation and creativity thrive.

3. Most teams that fail suffer one of five team dysfunctions: lack of trust, fear of conflict, lack of commitment, avoidance of accountability, and inattention to results.

4. The success of most teams can be predicted based on their composition. A strong team should have a mix of personality types, strong social skills, and a significant number of women to be successful.

5. Building trust among group members, both in terms of trust in the group and trust in your organization, is essential.

6. A team with a clearly defined goal is far more likely to excel than one with a nebulous or poorly defined goal.

7. The roles of team members must be articulated and defined so that there is no confusion about job responsibilities. In-team bickering wastes time and destroys productivity.

15
Using Psychology to Influence Culture

We believe that it's really important to come up with core values that you can commit to. And by commit, we mean that you're willing to hire and fire based on them. If you're willing to do that, then you're well on your way to building a company culture that is in line with the brand you want to build.

~ Tony Hsieh, CEO of Zappos.com

A company is more than just a building or a collection of people who work there. Whether you have consciously thought about it or not, your company or department has a culture—a way of thinking and acting that affects each employee as well as the perception other people have of your organization. Corporate culture has a direct effect on your success as a company, and can also help potential employees decide whether or not they want to work for you. If you're not taking time to build a healthy and vibrant culture for your company, then you should rethink your management strategy.

What Is Organizational Culture?

Organizational culture may feel like a nebulous idea. If so, remember that it's a collection of only three parts—beliefs, norms, and values. Each of these parts helps to characterize the organization as a whole, and is broken down as follows:[1]

- **The beliefs** of an organization include beliefs about the best way to achieve organizational goals. Beliefs are specific statements that people hold to be true. For example, leaders might believe that well-rounded employees who take recovery breaks and make time for leisure are more productive than overworked employees.

- **The norms** of an organization are the typical and accepted behaviors. For example, one norm might be that the working atmosphere at an organization is relaxed and open. Another norm might reflect the manner of making decisions or even company policies such as regular meetings. As an example, the belief might be that recovery breaks are important and the norm is that people take recovery breaks.

- **The values** of an organization go to what is most important to the organization as a whole. They are the social principles, goals and standards about what is good and bad. For example, an organization might place a high premium on creativity, innovation, teamwork, and community service. Those values serve to inform the behavior and mindset of employees at every level.

Let's look at some examples of different company cultures.

1. Southwest Airlines has a reputation for being different from other airlines. Their culture is characterized by giving employees the freedom to go above and beyond what's expected to make customers happy. They value originality and reward people for having a fun-loving nature. This reflects in the cheerful attitude of employees.

2. REI, an American retail and outdoor recreation services company, has tied its corporate culture to its products. Environmental protection is one of the organization's core values, and they encourage employees to come up with adventures using the equipment they sell. REI also believes in connecting with the outdoors and so they offer staff a 'Yay Day'. This company paid day is an opportunity for staff to challenge themselves in a favourite activity or reconnect with the outdoors. The aim is to reward and energize staff but also prepare staff to deliver great knowledge and service to customers.

3. As an organization, Adobe values autonomy. They believe this value can be met by allowing employees to set their own goals. They normalize this belief by giving employees this privilege and having managers act as coaches, providing guidance and support to ensure that those employee-created goals are met.[2]

As you can see, each of these companies not only has a unique culture, but also makes the different aspects of culture work together. Research shows a direct correlation between company culture and performance. A 1992 study, for example, looked at the organizational culture of 11 insurance companies and found that those companies with a clearly defined culture outperformed those companies that had not articulated their culture.[3]

Let's look at another example...

Case Study – Zappos.com

The organizational culture at Zappos.com is illustrative of why culture is so closely tied to success.

You might think of Zappos as an online shoe retailer, but CEO Tony Hsieh would disagree. He sees Zappos as a great customer service company... which happens to sell shoes and other apparel.[4]

Zappos makes a big deal about corporate culture. In the early days after Hsieh joined the company, he interviewed every employee himself. He knew he wanted an atmosphere that was fun and creative, and he hired employees based on those criteria. He asked himself, *"Is this a person I would want to know outside of work?"* Gradually, the company got too big for him to interview everybody, but he communicated the culture to his subordinates knowing that they would make hiring decisions using the same criteria.

In fact, Zappos made their 10 core values and hiring criteria public.[5] They include:

- Deliver WOW through service
- Embrace and drive change
- Build open and honest relationships with communication
- Be adventurous, creative, and open-minded

Zappos' organizational culture is clearly defined at every level, from its CEO all the way down to employees who answer the phones. There are hundreds, if not thousands, of stories in circulation about how Zappos employees have embraced this culture to deliver fantastic experiences to their customers, including several about customers receiving flowers or pizza late at night.

Psychological Principles to Develop Positive Organizational Culture

What are the psychological principles leaders can use to develop a positive organizational culture—one that will create an environment that encourages success?

1. **Habits**. Five monkeys are put in a cage with a ladder, on which is a bunch of bananas.[7] Each time a monkey scales the ladder to get a banana, the scientists outside the cage douse the remaining monkeys with water. Within a short period of time, all the monkeys beat up any other monkey that goes after the bananas. Eventually, one of the monkeys is replaced with a new monkey who immediately goes for the bananas. He is beaten by the other monkeys, and very quickly learns not to climb the ladder even though he was never doused with water. The pattern continues until all of the monkeys in the cage are new. Despite the fact that they have no idea why the beatings happen, they all participate.

    This story isn't factual. Though, like most fables, it has its roots in reality. In this case, the story is based upon experiments conducted on rhesus monkeys in 1965.[6] What both the fable and the original rhesus-monkey experiments tell us is that corporate culture can develop as a matter of habit. These habits you want to influence, otherwise you risk not arriving at the culture you want, which is one that's tied to company values. The lesson here is also that changing culture is not simply a matter of adding or taking away one person. I have witnessed the dismissal of "problem" employees—employees exhibiting bullying behavior, for example—only to witness another, remaining employee exhibit the same learned behavior despite the original employee no longer being in the company. Shifting company culture takes time and requires targeted changes, including defining, guiding, and rewarding desired habits and behaviors.

2. **Value, rarity, and inimitability.** A 1986 study on the impact of corporate culture on financial performance found that a culture must have three attributes in order to feed financial success.[8] First, the culture has to be valuable—it must enable employees to do things that add value, such as attracting new customers and innovating products. Second, the culture must be rare—it must not be too similar to the culture of any other organization. Third, it must not be easily imitable—other organizations should not be able to piggyback on your culture as a way of duplicating your success.

3. **Corporate-culture based hiring.** A good predictor of how newly hired employees will perform is how well

they fit into the corporate culture. A 1991 study showed that person/culture fit was essential in hiring quality employees who perform well within a culture.[9] As you might expect, there is also a negative correlation, meaning that companies that hire without regard for person/culture fit end up having high employee dissatisfaction and turnover, both of which can be costly and impact the company's bottom line.

Applications for Your Organization

So, what can you do as a leader to use these psychological principles to enhance your company culture?

1. **Audit corporate culture.** Conducting regular corporate-culture audits can help ensure that the way you are doing things still has relevance. Remember the fable about the monkeys. By the time all of the monkeys in the cage had been replaced, none of them had any idea why climbing the ladder resulted in a beating. It became a matter of doing things for no better reason than that's the way it had always been done. If there are procedures or cultural standards that nobody understands, that's a good indication that it's time to re-examine them. You may end up deciding to keep them after all, but you should do so only if you can clearly define why you need them.

2. **Start with employees**. If you find that you have a difficult time defining your company's culture—or if you haven't yet made an effort to do so—your employees are the best place to start. What do they want from the culture? What things are missing and what things do they already like? Remember, to be successful, an organization's culture must be embraced by everybody. Asking employees about it is a good place to start.

3. **Communicate the culture clearly and consistently**. Whether you are defining your culture for the first time, attempting to redefine it, or simply wanting to get everybody on the same page, it's your job as a leader to communicate your culture clearly to employees. Many companies, including Zappos, have a written statement about corporate culture. It's on their website and something that every employee understands. However, you must do more than define your organizational culture if you want it to take hold. You must also embody it for your employees. If they see you embracing the ideals you have articulated, then they will embrace them too.

4. **Hire with culture in mind**. Don't make the mistake of assuming that a skilled employee will be a good fit for your culture. Everybody in the hiring process should be aware that culture is front and center when it comes

to hiring. Remember, cultural fit is a better predictor of job performance and satisfaction than are skills, so don't gloss over this aspect of the hiring process. Find employees who can embrace your culture easily and your organization will reap the rewards.

The primary thing that you must remember about culture is that it is—and should be—truly indicative of your organization's values, beliefs, and goals. It should permeate the workplace in the way that Zappos' culture does, with each employee understanding that everybody—from the CEO's office down to the loading dock—is working toward the same shared values. When that happens, financial success will follow.

Key Takeaways

1. Organizational culture is defined by a set of shared beliefs, norms, and values that serve as guiding principles for every employee at every level.

2. There is a direct link between corporate culture and financial success. Companies that have a well-defined culture perform better than companies that do not.

3. A good organizational culture is one that is valuable, rare, and not easily imitable. It's not enough to mimic another company's culture. Your organization's culture must be a true reflection of your core values and mindset.

4. A culture that fosters creative problem solving is likely to create reliable results even when systems break down or equipment fails. When employees share clearly defined values and goals and understand company objectives, they strive to meet them at all times, especially when conditions are not ideal.

5. Hiring employees based on how they fit with your culture is the best predictor of future job performance and employee satisfaction—more so than skills, training, or education. Your culture should be your first consideration when making hiring decisions.

16
The Psychology of Change

Some people don't like change, but you need to embrace change if the alternative is disaster.
~ Elon Musk

Resistance to change is part of being human. All of us have moments when we feel the ground shifting beneath our feet and wish that we could find a way to stop it. As a leader though, it is part of your responsibility to embrace change when it is necessary, and to help employees embrace it as well.

What Is Change?

For patients who are in therapy, psychologists define change as the patient moving from dysfunctional behavior to functional behavior.[1] When thinking about a workplace situation, it makes sense to think of the old way of doing things as representing dysfunctional behavior, and the new way of doing them as functional behavior.

In other words, when an organization states that there is a need for change, what its leaders are saying is that the currently accepted norms are no longer sufficient, and that the time has come to evaluate and revamp them in some way. The challenge for leaders in such a situation is to convey the need for change to employees in a way that they will embrace the change wholeheartedly and do what is needed to make it happen.

Change comes to an organization in many different guises. Some changes are relatively straightforward, such as the change from an obsolete computer program to a new one. Others, such as changing a major aspect of customer service or employee functions, may be dramatic and require a great deal of adaptation on the part of employees.

The ability to shepherd your organization and employees through major changes is essential. Even if you have a company that is highly functional right now, change is inevitable. All things evolve. Changes in the outside world, technology, and the economy—to name just a few—will require your organization to evolve in response to those external changes.[2]

Case Study – Nokia

Perhaps no company in the world better illustrates the necessity of change than Nokia. The company is 150 years old, and has reinvented itself a number of times. The most recent transformation happened as the company's leaders realized that its mobile phone division, which had formerly been a dominating force in the industry, was no longer economically viable.[3]

CEO Risto Siilasmaa knew that the company would have to make bold changes to survive. He saw an opportunity in their partnership with Siemens, which focused on manufacturing and selling network equipment. He accomplished the company's evolution with two decisive moves. First, he sold the company's mobile division to Microsoft. Second, he bought Siemens out of their partnership and made networking the company's new focus.

Those changes had a ripple effect that required additional transformations. Before long, Nokia had a new corporate structure and a new management team. Since making the changes, the value of the company's stock has increased dramatically.

What can leaders learn from Nokia's experience? The first lesson is that no organization can avoid change. The world is always evolving and the survivors are those who evolve with it. The second lesson is that change is not something to be feared. Finally, realize that incremental changes may not be enough in some situations. When that is the case, effective leaders make bold moves and dramatic changes, keeping the overall interests of the organization in mind.

Psychological Principles to Lead Change

The key to affecting change as a leader is to understand what change is, and then to use the proper tools to navigate it, helping employees along the way. Change has profound effects on the brain and it's important to understand what they are. With that in mind, let's talk about some psychological principles that can help.

1. **Neuroscience.** To understand why change is so difficult, we should look to the science of the brain. When we are presented with new situations, the amygdala (part of the limbic system) does a rapid search to see if the present situation resembles anything that has caused us to feel fearful, angry, or threatened in the past. If it does, the amygdala kicks into "fight or flight" mode, triggering something called the "amygdala hijack."[4] When our brains have been hijacked by the amygdala, we tend to have strong and sometimes irrational emotional reactions, which can impede our ability to accept change.

    a. **The amygdala**. The reaction of the human brain to a threat is a binary one. When the amygdala assesses a situation, it decides one of two things:

that there is no danger, or that there is danger.[5] It doesn't worry about the type of danger, which means that it is unable to differentiate between a mortal threat and a threat posed by a proposed change.

b. **Habits.** Habits are formed in the basal ganglia, which is also part of the limbic system.[6] When we are presented with any complex situation, it requires less energy and effort to revert to a habit than it does to embrace the idea of change and move forward. If we are to change, the prefrontal cortex must engage in complex thought, and that requires energy and resources. For example, a person who wants to change their eating habits must fight against cravings, which can be identified as a form of stress. It is far easier to give into the craving and eat something than it is to resist. This is why it is so hard for the brain to accept change.

2. **The SCARF model.** Learning how to approach change is essential. One psychological tool that will help is the SCARF model.[7] It looks at five areas of importance: status, certainty, autonomy, relatedness, and fairness, and it can tell us quite a bit about why people react with fear when presented with change.

a. **Status**. A 2003 study showed that the experience of having one's status threatened or lowered affects the body in the same way as physical pain.[8] Research shows that a threat to someone's status is perceived, psychologically speaking, in the same way as a threat to their life. This means that, if people feel that their status is being threatened, then they will likely show resistance to change and react negatively. An example of this is when there is a new CEO. This change means that the leadership team will have to build relationships with a new boss. But proving themselves and their value to the organization means their status is threatened. Sometimes, negative behaviors and mindsets are brought out. Another example is the change of someone's job tasks or job title, in which they might perceive the change as reducing their level of responsibility. In the brain this invokes the threat response and makes it more difficult for the individual to accept and embrace the change. Instead, when people feel that their status is protected, they are more likely to respond positively to change.

b. **Certainty**. We're all hardwired to value certainty, particularly when it comes to being able to predict the outcome of events. When we feel uncertain, error messages that impair our ability to think clearly are sent to the brain.[9] This is why, when it comes to managing change, we need to communicate, communicate, communicate. It is better to over-communicate than under-communicate. Provide staff with certainty when you can, so that they are not left making incorrect assumptions and filling in the gaps themselves—causing more damage as rumors fly.

c. **Autonomy**. There is a direct link between health and loss of autonomy and control.[10] Adult humans are hardwired to be independent, and any sense that control is being lost can have a detrimental effect. Delegate and give trust and responsibility to people. Train your leadership and management groups to do the same. The management level tends to be the group that micromanages and has difficulty allowing autonomy.

d. **Relatedness**. Human beings make very quick judgments about whether other people are friends or foes.[11] When there is no sense of relatedness, our brains react with fear and mistrust. This is why building relationships and trust is critical.

e. **Fairness**. When we perceive something as being unfair, we react with strong emotions like anger and disgust.[12] Fairness, in contrast, lights up the reward centers in our brains and makes us feel valued. How do you reduce perceptions of unfairness? Make sure that you and your entire leadership group are making consistent, equitable, and fair decisions. No one should receive special treatment. Have fair and clear processes, policies, and delegations. Promote the company's fair practices. For example, with recruitment decisions, staff will want to know that merit-based and fair recruitment processes occur rather than people being promoted because they have connections or are next in line.

The key is to approach change—and help others approach it—willingly, instead of sending them the cues that will spark their threat response.

3. **Cognitive dissonance** occurs any time there is a discrepancy between what happens to people and what they believe to be true.[13] Cognitive dissonance is why people can experience mental distress or discomfort when an action is performed, or new information provided, that is contrary to their beliefs, ideas, or values. People will act to reduce this dissonance and avoid situations and information that are likely to increase it.

An example of cognitive dissonance in the workplace is a person being asked to perform tasks that are not in line with standard procedures or norms. The person's internal sense of right or wrong is placed against the expectations of the senior decision maker and the potential negative impact on their career if they say no. This causes cognitive dissonance and can result in a high level of stress for the individual.

Another example can be when there is a choice between more than one option. If the option chosen by the organization, manager or another party, does not align with what the employee believes to be the best approach or option, then the employee can experience cognitive dissonance. As a result, they may downplay the benefits of the rejected option.

Cognitive dissonance in a workplace causes absenteeism, disengagement, reductions in performance, turnover, health and wellness issues, negativity, and inappropriate behavior. This is why it is important for leaders to recognize and minimize cognitive dissonance through clearly defined organizational processes and practices.

4. **Reinforcement** is essential when it comes to getting people to embrace and carry out changes.[14] Leaders who announce changes once and expect them to

occur are bound to be disappointed, whereas those who make a concerted effort to follow up and offer positive reinforcement to workers are likely to see their changes implemented successfully.

These principles provide insight into the way the brain responds to change and why change is naturally difficult for people.

Applications for Your Organization

How can leaders use psychology to ensure that the changes they need to make are embraced by employees and carried out appropriately?

1. **Educate staff.** Educate staff on the neuroscience of change. Change for the brain is difficult. So, it is okay that people experience an initial resistance to change. Some people require more time than others. We all experience different emotions in response to change and different people react more strongly to different types of changes. Educate staff on the emotion curve, use the SCARF model to reduce threats, and support staff so that they can process change more quickly.

2. **Get feedback.** Getting feedback from your employees early in the change process will help you gauge what stage of acceptance staff is in. It will also help you to

engage the group and give staff permission to be part of the change journey. You don't have to take every suggestion, but when team members feel that their voices have been heard and their suggestions valued, they are far more likely to get on board with changes than they would otherwise be.

3. **Give employees a clear motive for change.** An individual who wants to make a personal change such as losing weight is likely to succeed if they feel that the benefits of doing so outweigh the risks of not doing it.[15] Spend some time explaining what you hope the changes will mean for the future, and do whatever you can to back up your assertions to reduce uncertainty.

4. **Consider an internal coaching program.** An internal coaching program can maximize the acceptance of proposed changes. Senior staff can take an active role in training rank-and-file employees, shepherding them through the changes.

5. **Give employees positive reinforcement.** As you move through the process of changing your organization, positive reinforcement can help employees accept change, and feel less threatened in their positions. When you use positive reinforcement well, it can serve as a way to decrease fears related to status changes as well as increasing certainty that the changes will be

beneficial both to employees and to the organization. Things like praising employees for their progress or announcing milestones can do a great deal to maintain momentum and keep morale high.

6. **Look for signs of cognitive dissonance.** Watch for symptoms of cognitive dissonance and, when found, do what you can to help employees resolve it. Major changes are likely to inspire some dissonance, particularly if employee roles are changing or you are restructuring. Be sensitive to the fact that perceived changes in status are likely to be met with resistance and find ways to reassure employees that their status will be positively impacted by the changes. If you are changing titles, make sure to explain them in such a way that employees see them (at worst) as a lateral move.

7. **Simplify the process.** An easy way to do this is by breaking down large goals into small, achievable steps—like what was covered in chapter 6 (Resilience), in the setting mini goals section. Change is often best achieved when it is implemented in increments. Think of it as training your employees. You can't expect somebody who's never gone running to complete a marathon simply because you told them to do so. Instead, supply employees with clear goals and the

training required to meet them. Each step they take should bring them (and your organization) closer to meeting your long-term goals without inspiring the fear and doubt that might be present if you expected the changes to happen all at once.

8. **Use team-building activities.** Social events and team-building activities can increase employees' sense of relatedness both to the change process and to one another. This type of activity is especially important if you are bringing in new employees or requiring current employees to work in newly formed teams. Having regular meetings and encouraging social interaction can help cement new relationships and minimize fears.

By following these steps and giving your employees the tools they need to navigate changes, you can greatly increase the likelihood that the changes will be successful.

Key Takeaways

1. Change is defined as moving from dysfunction (the old, ineffective way of doing things) to function (the new, efficient way of doing things).

2. Human beings are hardwired to look at change with fear and anxiety. Your job as a leader is to mitigate your employees' fear and shepherd them through the changes.

3. Thanks to the amygdala hijack, significantly less effort is required to maintain the status quo than to make a change.

4. Change is inevitable, and your ability to navigate change is essential to your success as a leader.

5. To help employees adjust, put changes into their proper context by explaining why they are necessary and outlining their benefits.

6. The more you do to protect status, provide certainty, allow autonomy, encourage relatedness, and project fairness, the more your employees will do to help you make the changes that need to be made.

7. Breaking big changes down into small milestones and goals is essential because it can make even the largest, most sweeping changes feel achievable. When employees are overwhelmed, they are likely to resist change out of fear.

17
The Psychology of Millennials

Millennials are more aware of society's many challenges than previous generations and less willing to accept maximizing shareholder value as a sufficient goal for their work. They are looking for a broader social purpose and want to work somewhere that has such a purpose.

~ Michael Porter

Every leader must learn how to manage their people. As convenient as it would be to use the same management techniques for every employee, reality is not that simple. People differ when it comes to the style of management that is best able to motivate and inspire them. However, there are commonalities within generations.

The millennial generation now makes up a significant percentage of the workforce. Because they differ from preceding generations in some significant ways, learning how their psychology differs and is similar to previous generations is very valuable.

What Are Millennials?

The term "millennial" was first coined by historians Neil Howe and William Strauss to describe people born between 1980 and 2000.[1] While the range of years is somewhat fluid, the generally accepted definition is that a millennial is someone who was born and came of age at approximately the same time that the 20th century turned into the 21st.

Defining a millennial in psychological terms is a bit more complex. Psychologically, millennials have some unique characteristics.[2]

- First, millennials are sometimes referred to as "digital natives" because they do not remember a time when computer use, mobile phones, and the internet weren't the norm.

- Second, and on a related note, millennials are very creative. In fact, more than 50% of all millennials are engaged in online content creation.

- Third, millennials tend to have a strong trust in organizations, thanks to growing up at a time when institutions (such as the government) intervened to try to improve education and give children opportunities.

- Fourth, millennials tend to be highly results driven (they are accustomed to competition) but also can require affirmation and feedback.

- Fifth, millennials tend to place a high premium on work-life balance, and demonstrate a high degree of loyalty to institutions they perceive to be flexible and adaptable to their needs. This trait often translates into a desire to work at their own pace and in their own way.
- Sixth, millennials tend to want enterprising careers, particularly those where the work they do has the potential to influence others.[3]

Managing Millennials

There are some distinguishing differences between the way millennials and other generations work. Differences that if understood and utilised, can be of great value to organizations and leaders.

Leaders who have been accustomed to managing baby boomers or generation Xers often find that their usual management style is less effective when it comes to managing millennials. Here are some of the most common differences that leaders face when managing this new generation of workers.

- **Paying dues**. It is common for Baby boomers to hold the perception that workers have to pay their dues, and that putting in long hours is part of career success. Millennials value work-life balance, as opposed to long work hours, and they have a strong focus on productivity and working more efficiently. For this reason, this can be a challenge for organizations to manage competing views and different career priorities between the different generations. For example, when baby boomers see millennials progressing up the ladder quickly. Or when millennials are viewed as lazy because they are less focused on the perception of long hours.[4]

- **Focus on self.** Millennials are sometimes referred to as the selfie generation, and the stereotypical perception is that they can be narcissistic and self-centered.[5] However, studies have directly contradicted the view that millennials are more self-centred or narcissistic that other generations. For example, Psychologists Trzesniewski and Donnellan conducted a large survey across multiple decades, finding no significant change across generations for egotism, self-enhancement, individualism or self-esteem.[6]

- **Expectations.** Some leaders complain that millennials have unrealistic expectations in terms of promotions and raises, with some leaving jobs after six months because they had not been rewarded adequately for the work they had done.[7] This attitude is anathema to people who grew up with the attitude that people have to pay their dues before advancing.

From the perspective of millennials, they tend to value efficiency, productivity and self-learning. Millennials tend to be always learning, on the job and outside of work. They often show self-respect and hold themselves to high standards. For these reasons, millennials typically believe that they should not have to wait the same amount of time as previous generations to prove that they can excel at higher levels. This links to their desire for recognition and feedback—they want to see the fruits of their labour. They are also less likely to stay put, if they view that they are not the right fit for the organization or are unhappy on the job.

- **Switching jobs**. Millennials' idea of careerism is another trait that differs from other generations.[8] Rather than staying with the same company for many years, millennials have a tendency to take a more cosmopolitan view of their careers. They often switch jobs more frequently in an effort to find the meaning and stimulation they crave. For organizations, this means motivating and engaging employees to gain the most from their time with the organization. It means preparing for turnover. It also means, lower risk of unhappy employees sticking around.

- **Attitude toward supervision.** Millennials' have a stronger preference for autonomy and influence. At the same time, they seek regular and timely feedback.[9] On the one hand, millennials are said to have grown up expecting to be in a nurturing and loving environment where they were given every possible tool for success. On the other hand, they value autonomy and want to be left to work at their own pace. When managing millennials, this means balancing nurturing and positive reinforcement with autonomy.

While millennials bring a new dimension to the current workplace, there are challenges with managing people from all different generations. Managers learned that the best way to manage baby boomers was to show them how they could be an organizational star, providing development opportunities and involving them in operational matters. Greatest generation expected conformity to rules and valued sacrifice. They were best managed by people of status where authority needed to be earned.

The key takeaway for organizations is to look past the stereotypes, take advantage of the opportunities that each generation brings, educate employees on working better together, and accommodating the generational mix in organizations today.

Why Working with Millennials Matters

According to research from Pew Charitable Trust, millennials are the most diverse and educated demographic. Millennials often have a strong desire to make an impact, they want to find meaning in their work and are intrinsically motivated. They bring untapped perspectives and innovative approaches. They collaborate, are inclusive in their style and generally great at teamwork. While they can be viewed as impatient, wanting everything right away, this makes millennials tenacious in the workplace, finding answers and getting things done quickly. They also tend to be highly driven, optimistic and very adaptable. [10]

Because of these reasons organizations like American Evaluation Association (AEA) are capitalizing on the value add of the millennial generation. Steward Donaldson, president of AEA, is known for prioritizing age diversity at AEA and engaging a millennial on the board. This appointment added value to AEA because the individual could "give us real insight to how her generational peers are impacted by our programs and decisions." AEA considers candidates by their potential as much as existing skill sets. Corrie Whitmore, AEA board member and millennial noted that "The traditional belief is that you cannot be on a board unless you have certain years of experience in the field or have served on certain committees. Well, people measure experience differently. Yes, I am in my

30s, but I am using new technology in ways my colleagues have not. I have had a number of roles in a few years where my peers have been in fewer roles for longer years. And along the way, I have earned a master's degree, defended a dissertation and started a family. That is a different — but relevant — kind of experience."[11]

Psychological Principles of Leading Millennials

Now let's look at some of the research around leading millennials, and how this research can help you in the workplace.

- **Work flexibility.** Research shows that an increase in the average time people spend working has actually led to a decrease in their desire to advance into leadership positions.[12] This is particularly true for millennials who value work-life balance. Organizations who are looking to attract millennials, at all levels in the business, need to consider their organizational beliefs and customs when it comes to work hours and work flexibility. Gear your benefits toward flexibility and rewards for a job well done. Millennials tend to appreciate things like flex time, telecommuting, and being rewarded with time off or other perks.

- **Feedback**. As compared to baby boomers and generation Xers, millennials have a strong need for feedback and appreciation.[13] Millennials expect regular feedback and encouragement. It's not enough to assume that your employees know that you appreciate them. Leaders must genuinely express feedback on a regular basis—even if doing so goes against the grain. Other generations will enjoy the extra appreciation, too. Remember, the generations are more alike than they are different.

- **Expression of needs**. When researchers looked at metrics such as job satisfaction and recognition, millennials were actually more satisfied than their predecessors.[14] This suggests that perhaps millennials are more likely to express their needs than earlier generations were, thus influencing their satisfaction. While other generations may not be as forward about their needs, you are more likely to know where you stand with millennials. As Laszlo Block, Human Resources Chief at Google noted, "The only thing different about [millennials] is that they are actually asking for the things that everybody else wants,"[15]

- **Loyalty**. Research shows that millennials tend to be extremely loyal when they are supported and engaged—something that bodes well for leaders who can provide an environment that encourages them.[16] Take for example, millennials' strong need to contribute. This is one way that you can engage millennials. In fact, a millennial employee at Intuit took charge of finding ways to make the company more creative and innovative. After spending hundreds of (unpaid) hours working on the idea, it was launched and it increased employee idea creation and advancement by 1000%—value for the organization and for the employee.[17] So, what can you do to capitalize on the drive and creativity of millennials working for you?

- **Altruism** and giving back to the community. Millennials tend to want to contribute to the community. Companies who encourage volunteerism, have a social cause and/or work with employees to allow altruism are more likely to attract millennials.

- **The work environment**. Millennials place a high premium on a fun and relaxed work environment.[18] In other words, if your company culture reflects a spirit of collaboration and flexibility, you are more likely to attract millennials. Companies like Google have done a good job showing prospective employees that their culture is a good fit by using video and other technologies to give them a peek behind the scenes.

- **Technology**. Millennials' skills in the areas of computers, technology, teamwork, and innovation make them desirable employees who can help move organizations forward.[19] Millennials' technological ease and know-how can help organizations move forward and grow, and organizations that harness this comfort with technology can reap significant benefits.

- **Similarities**. While there are differences, there are also many points of similarity between millennials and previous generations. Mencl and Lester conducted research on what generations' value in the workplace. Their research indicated consistent similarities among baby boomers, millennials and generation X employees currently in the workforce. Results demonstrated significant similarities showing that all three generations valued teamwork, having a job that challenges them, a company that provides continual training and development opportunities, and being involved in decision making processes that affect their work.[20]

Organizations will benefit from educating staff on similarities between generations, cultures, age and other diversity factors. Education aids organizational acceptance, understanding and cohesion.

The key takeaway for organizations is that there are key values and beliefs that attract, engage and retain millennials, but there are also many similarities between the different generations. This means that you do not have to upend the organization to attract and engage millennials. Instead targeted strategies will help you reap the rewards from all generations.

Case Study - General Electric

In 2012, General Electric decided to take a methodical approach to attracting millennials and finding ways to harness their unique talents. They convened a 21-person team of millennials from various divisions of their organization to form the company's strategy for hiring and inspiring millennials.[21] They made several key recommendations:

- Create a suite of flexible benefits to help millennials achieve the work-life balance they crave.
- Provide more just-in-time feedback and support. This is timely, on the job, task specific feedback.
- Expand leadership development programs to help millennials grow with the organization.
- Use gaming technology to teach potential employees about the organization and its values.

Instead of resisting the idea of hiring millennials, GE decided to embrace it and find ways to work with them.

Case Study - Jared's

Jared's is a popular chain of restaurants that started on the East Coast of the United States and has now expanded into a global company. The company's expansion led to significant changes in terms of employee workloads, and the company worked hard to offer flexibility in the form of reduced work hours.[22] One employee had originally cut back her time by 20% but still found that she was overwhelmed. Her pay had been set at 80% of her original salary, but she felt resentful because she was really working at about 90% of what she had been doing before, so she felt undercompensated.

On the verge of resigning, she scheduled a meeting with her manager. The manager did not want to lose her, so they worked together to agree upon a 50% schedule at 60% of her original salary—an acknowledgement of the fact that she would likely have to work more than half time to get her job done. They also hired an assistant to pick up the slack. The result was that both the manager and the employee were happy, and the employee went on to win a prestigious Employee of the Year award working her new, reduced hours.

These anecdotes show some of the possible benefits, both in employee loyalty and job performance, for companies that embrace the idea of working with millennials.

Working with Millennials requires a bit of a paradigm shift for leaders. However, the bottom line is that the psychology of millennials is not different so much as it is differently expressed. A leader who understands that will be successful when it comes to leading cross-generational organizations.

Key Takeaways

1. Millennials were born between 1980 and 2000, and will make up a majority of the workforce by 2026.
2. The defining characteristics of millennials include digital nativism, respect for organizations, a desire for work-life balance, a need for approval, and a desire to make a difference in the world.
3. Leaders tend to view millennials as lazy, self-centered, needy, and unrealistic.
4. Millennials are computer natives, meaning that they do not remember a time when computer use was not the norm. They are very comfortable with technology and can help organizations move into the future.
5. Millennials put a high premium on corporate culture, and value a workplace that emphasizes fun and innovation.
6. A company that offers flexibility in terms of work hours is likely to be attractive to millennials.

7. Millennials have a strong need for feedback and appreciation, and are likely to express that need more forcefully than other generations might.

Conclusion

I'd like to thank you for reading. I hope you have gained some interesting insights into what makes you as a leader, and those under your guidance, tick. At its basic level, leadership really is an exercise in understanding human nature.

To that end, it is my hope that the findings herein will, in some small way, shape your leadership approach moving forward.

Citations

Chapter 1: The Psychology of Decision Making

1. The worst business decisions of all time. (2012, October 17). Retrieved from http://247wallst.com/special-report/2012/10/17/the-worst-business-decisions-of-all-time/2/
2. Kahneman, D. (2011). *Thinking, fast and slow*. Macmillan.
3. Kahneman, D. (2011). *Thinking, fast and slow*. Macmillan.
4. Samuelson, W., & Zeckhauser, R. (1988). Status quo bias in decision making. *Journal of Risk and Uncertainty*, *1*(1), 7-59.
5. Knox, R. E., & Inkster, J. A. (1968). Post Decision Dissonance at Post Time 1. *Journal of Personality and Social Psychology, 8*(4), 319-323.
6. (2015, August). Retrieved from http://www.afr.com/technology/in-1975-this-kodak-employee-invented-the-digital-camera-his-bosses-made-him-hide-it-20150813-k9zo8
7. Ohno, T. (2006). Ask why five time about every matter. Retrieved from http://www.toyota-global.com/company/toyota_traditions/quality/mar_apr_2006.html

8. Kahneman, D., & Tversky, A. (1984). Choices, values, and frames. *American Psychologist, 39*(4), 341.

Chapter 2: Using Psychology to Build Credibility

1. Covey, S. M. R. (2009) *How the best leaders build trust.* Retrieved from http://www.leadershipnow.com/CoveyOnTrust.html
2. McGarry, J., & Hendrick, C. (1974). Communicator credibility and persuasion. Memory & Cognition, 2(1), 82-86.
3. Gabris, G. T., & Ihrke, D. M. (2000). Improving employee acceptance toward performance appraisal and merit pay systems: The role of leadership credibility. Review of Public Personnel Administration, 20(1), 41-53.
4. Gabris, G. T., Golembiewski, R. T., & Ihrke, D. M. (2001). Leadership credibility, board relations, and administrative innovation at the local government level. Journal of Public Administration Research and Theory, 11(1), 89-108.
5. Murray, R. (2013, December 4). A timeline of Lululemon controversy. Retrieved from http://www.nydailynews.com/life-style/timeline-lululemon-controversy-article-1.1536169
6. Murray, R. (2013, December 4). A timeline of Lululemon controversy. Retrieved from http://www.nydailynews.com/life-style/timeline-lululemon-controversy-article-1.1536169

7. Lee, F., & Tiedens, L. Z. (2001). Who's being served? "Self-serving" attributions in social hierarchies. Organizational Behavior and Human Decision Processes, 84(2), 254-287.
8. Michaely, R., & Womack, K. L. (1999). Conflict of interest and the credibility of underwriter analyst recommendations. Review of Financial Studies, 12(4), 653-686.
9. Salwen, M. B. (1987). Credibility of newspaper opinion polls: Source, source intent and precision. Journalism & Mass Communication Quarterly, 64(4), 813-819.
10. Kouzes, J.M., & Posner, B.Z. (2011). Credibility: How leaders gain and lose it, why people demand it (Vol. 244) 13-19.
11. Figuieres, C., Masclet, D., & Willinger, M. (2012). Vanishing leadership and declining reciprocity in a sequential contribution experiment. Economic Inquiry, 50(3), 567-584.
12. Kouzes, J. M., & Posner, B. Z. (2011). Credibility: How leaders gain and lose it, why people demand it (Vol. 244). John Wiley & Sons.

Chapter 3: Using Psychology to Influence and Persuade

1. Cialdini, R. B. (1987). *Influence: The psychology of persuasion*. Collins.

2. Perloff, R. M. (2003). The dynamics of persuasion. Communication and attitude in the 21st century. Hillsdale, NJ: LawrencelbErbaum.
3. Cialdini, R. B. (1987). Influence: The psychology of persuasion. Collins.
4. Regan, D. T. (1971). Effects of a favor and liking on compliance. Journal of Experimental Social Psychology, 7(6), 627-639.
5. Moriarty, T. (1975). Crime, commitment, and the responsive bystander: Two field experiments. Journal of Personality and Social Psychology, 31(2), 370.
6. Greenwald, A. G., Carnot, C. G., Beach, R., Young, B. (1987). Increasing voting behaviour by asking people if they expect to vote. Journal of Applied Psychology, 72(2), 315 – 318.
7. Milgram, S. (1963). Behavioral study of obedience. The Journal of Abnormal and Social Psychology, 67(4), 371.
8. Efrain, M. G., & Patterson, E. W. J. (1974). Voters vote beautiful: The effect of physical appearance on a national election. Canadian Journal of Behavioural Science/Revue Canadienne des Sciences du Comportement, 6(4), 352.
9. Emswiller, T., Deaux, K., & Willits, J. E. (1971). Similarity, sex, and requests for small favors 1. Journal of Applied Social Psychology, 1(3), 284-291.

10. Howard, D. J., Gengler, C., & Jain, A. (1995). What's in a name? A complementary means of persuasion. Journal of Consumer Research, 200-211.
11. Cialdini, R. B. (1987). Influence: The psychology of persuasion. Collins.
12. Cioffi, D., & Garner, R. (1996). On doing the decision: Effects of active versus passive choice on commitment and self-perception. Personality and Social Psychology Bulletin, 22(2), 133-147.

Chapter 4: The Psychology of Modesty and Humility in Leaders

1. Harvey, J. H., & Pauwels, B. G. (2004). Modesty, humility, character strength, and positive psychology. *Journal of Social and Clinical Psychology, 23(5)*, 620-623.
2. Driver, J. (1989). The virtues of ignorance. *The Journal of Philosophy*, 373-384.
3. McMullin, I. (2010). A modest proposal: Accounting for the Virtuousness of modesty. The Philosophical Quarterly, 60(241), 783-807.
4. Banerjee, R. (2000). The development of an understanding of modesty. British Journal of Developmental Psychology, 18(4), 499-517.
5. Koenig, L. J. (1997, August). Depression and the cultural context of the self-serving bias. In Emory Symposia in Cognition, 7, pp. 62-74. Cambridge University Press.

6. Barron, L. G., & Sackett, P. R. (2008). Asian variability in performance rating modesty and leniency bias. Human Performance, 21(3), 277-290.
7. Davis, D. E., Worthington Jr, E. L., Hook, J. N., Emmons, R. A., Hill, P. C., Bollinger, R. A., & Van Tongeren, D. R. (2013). Humility and the development and repair of social bonds: Two longitudinal studies. Self and Identity, 12(1), 58-77.
8. Davis, D. E., Worthington Jr, E. L., Hook, J. N., Emmons, R. A., Hill, P. C., Bollinger, R. A., & Van Tongeren, D. R. (2013). Humility and the development and repair of social bonds: Two longitudinal studies. Self and Identity, 12(1), 58-77.
9. Catmull, E., & Wallace, A. (2014). *Creativity, Inc. Overcoming the unseen forces that stand in the way of truc inspiration.* New York: Random House, 200, 368.
10. Bloomfield, D., & Buhayar, N. (2015, March 13). Buffett follows 'avarice' warning by keeping $100,000 salary. Retrieved from http://www.bloomberg.com/news/articles/2015-03-13/buffett-follows-avarice-warning-by-sticking-to-100-000-salary
11. Schawbel, D. (2014, September 23). Richard Branson's three most important leadership principles. Retrieved from http://www.forbes.com/sites/danschawbel/2014/09/23/richard-branson-his-3-most-important-leadership-principles/#59eee1275ccf

12. Gardezi, F., Lingard, L., Espin, S., Whyte, S., Orser, B., & Baker, G. R. (2009). Silence, power and communication in the operating room. *Journal of Advanced Nursing*, *65*(7), 1390-1399.

Chapter 5: The Psychology of Power

1. Reicher, S. D., Haslam, S. A., & Platow, M. J. (2007). The new psychology of leadership. *Scientific American Mind*, *18*(4), 22-29.
2. French, J. R., Raven, B., & Cartwright, D. (1959). The bases of social power. Classics of OrganizationTtheory, 311-320.
3. Greene, C. N., & Podsakoff, P. M. (1981). Effects of withdrawal of a performance-contingent reward on supervisory influence and power. Academy of Management Journal, 24(3), 527-542.
4. Maner, J. K., & Mead, N. L. (2010). The essential tension between leadership and power: When leaders sacrifice group goals for the sake of self-interest. Journal of Personality and Social Psychology, 99(3), 482.
5. Maner, J. K., & Mead, N. L. (2010). The essential tension between leadership and power: when leaders sacrifice group goals for the sake of self-interest. Journal of Personality and Social Psychology, 99(3), 482.
6. Kifer, Y., Heller, D., Perunovic, W. Q. E., & Galinsky, A. (March, 2013). The good life of the powerful: The

experience of power and authenticity enhances subjective well-being. Psychological Science, 24(3).
7. McClelland, D. C., & Burnham, D. H. (1976). Power is the great motivator. Harvard Business Review, 54(2), 100-110.
8. Hambrick, D. C., & Finkelstein, S. (1987). Managerial discretion: A bridge between polar views of organizational outcomes. Research in Organizational Behavior, 9, 369-406.
9. Murphy, M. J., & Wright, D. W. (2005). Supervisees' perspectives of power use in supervision. Journal of Marital and Family Therapy, 31(3), 283-295.
10. Pfeffer, J., & Drummond, D. (2010). *Power: Why some people have it and others don't*. New York, NY: HarperBusiness.
11. Shipman, A. S. (2011). When confidence is detrimental: Influcnce of overconfidence on leadership effectiveness. The Leadership Quarterly, 22(4), 649-665.
12. Pfeffer, J., & Drummond, D. (2010). Power: Why some people have it and others don't. New York, NY: HarperBusiness.
13. Pfeffer, J., & Drummond, D. (2010). Power: Why some people have it and others don't. New York, NY: HarperBusiness.
14. Grimaldi, J. V. (1997, July 08). Starbucks CEO consoles slaying victims' families - coffee chain tightens security at D.C.-area stores. Retrieved May 06, 2016.

15. Ensley, M. D., Hmieleski, K. M., & Pearce, C. L. (2006). The importance of vertical and shared leadership within new venture top management teams: Implications for the performance of startups. The Leadership Quarterly, 17(3), 217-231.
16. Leithwood, K. A., & Poplin, M. S. (1992). Transformational leadership. Educational Leadership, 49, 5.
17. Waugh, W. L., & Streib, G. (2006). Collaboration and leadership for effective emergency management. *Public Administration Review, 66*(s1), 131-140.
18. Dowding, K. M. (1991). Rational choice and political power. Edward Elgar Pub.
19. Sharp, G. (1994). *The role of power in nonviolent struggle*. Boston, MA: Albert Einstein Institution.
20. Kraus, B. (2014). Introducing a model for analyzing the possibilities of power, help and control. *Social Work & Society, 12*(1).

Chapter 6: Using Psychology to Build of Resilience

1. Meichenbaum, D. (2007). Important facts about resilience: a consideration of research findings about resilience and implications for assessment and treatment. Melissa Institute. Retrieved from http://melissainstitute.com/documents/facts_resilience.pdf

2. Clarke, J., & Nicholson, J. (2010). Resilience: bounce back from whatever life throws at you. Crimson Publishing.
3. Clarke, J., & Nicholson, J. (2010). Resilience: bounce back from whatever life throws at you. Crimson Publishing.
4. Clarke, J., & Nicholson, J. (2010). Resilience: bounce back from whatever life throws at you. Crimson Publishing.
5. Werner, E. E., & Smith, R. S. (1992). Overcoming the odds: High risk children from birth to adulthood. Cornell University Press.
6. Dweck, C. (2006). Mindset: The new psychology of success. Random House.
7. Clarke, J., & Nicholson, J. (2010). Resilience: bounce back from whatever life throws at you. Crimson Publishing
8. Clarke, J., & Nicholson, J. (2010). Resilience: bounce back from whatever life throws at you. Crimson Publishing
9. Clarke, J., & Nicholson, J. (2010). Resilience: bounce back from whatever life throws at you. Crimson Publishing
10. Kraemer, H. (2015, June 18). How Ford CEO Alan Mullaly turned a broken company into the industry's comeback kid. Retrieved from http://qz.com/431078/how-ford-ceo-alan-mullaly-turned-a-broken-company-into-the-industrys-comeback-kid/
11. Ibarra-Coronado, E. G., Velazquez-Moctezuma, J., Diaz, D. Becerril-Villanueva, L. E., Pavon, L., & Morales-Montor, J. (2015). Sleep deprivation induces changes in immunity

in trichinella spiralis-infected rats. International Journal of Biological Science, 11(8), 901–912.

12. Landrigan, C. P., Rothschild, J. M., Cronin, J. W., Kaushal, R., Burdick, E., Katz, J. T., Lilly, C. M., Stone, P., Lockley, S. W. Bates, D. W., & Czeisler, C. A. (2004). Effect of reducing interns' work hours on serious medical errors in intensive care units. *The New England Journal of Medicine, 351*, 1838-1848.

13. Duckworth, A. L., Peterson, C., Matthews, M. D., & Kelly, D. R. (2007). Grit: Perseverance and passion for long-term goals. *Journal of Personality and Social Psychology, 92*(6), 1087-1101.

Chapter 7: The Psychology of Emotional Intelligence

1. Goleman, D. (2006). *Emotional intelligence*. Bantam.
2. Goleman, D. (2006). Emotional intelligence. Bantam.
3. George, J. M. (2000). Emotions and leadership: The role of emotional intelligence. Human Relations, 53(8), 1027-1055.
4. Goleman, D., Boyatzis, R. E., & McKee, A. (2001, December). Primal leadership: The hidden driver of great performance. Retrieved from https://hbr.org/2001/12/primal-leadership-the-hidden-driver-of-great-performance

5. Measuring the return on character. (2015, April). Retrieved from https://hbr.org/2015/04/measuring-the-return-on-character
6. Measuring the return on character. (2015, April). Retrieved from https://hbr.org/2015/04/measuring-the-return-on-character
7. Gilkey, R., Caceda, R., & Kilts, C. (2010, September). When emotional reasoning trumps IQ. Retrieved from https://hbr.org/2010/09/when-emotional-reasoning-trumps-iq
8. Gardner, L., & Stough, C. (2002). Examining the relationship between leadership and emotional intelligence in senior level managers. Leadership & Organization Development Journal, 23(2), 68-78.
9. George, J. M. (2000). Emotions and leadership: The role of emotional intelligence. Human Relations, 53(8), 1027-1055.
10. Nadler, R. S. (2011). Leading with emotional intelligence. McGraw-Hill Education
11. Lynn, A. B. (2004). The EQ difference: A powerful plan for putting emotional intelligence to work. AMACOM Div American Mgmt Assn.
12. Nadler, R. S. (2011). Leading with emotional intelligence.
13. Anders, G. (2012, April 04). Jeff Bezos reveals his No. 1 leadership secret. Retrieved from http://www.forbes.com/forbes/2012/0423/ceo-compensation-12-amazon-technology-jeff-bezos-gets-it.html

14. 'Bezos rules Amazon employees with ice water in his veins' (2013). Retrieved from http://mynorthwest.com/5017/bezos-rules-amazon-employees-with-ice-water-in-his-veins/

15. Palmer, B. R., Stough, C., Harmer, R., & Gignac, G. (2009). The Genos Emotional Intelligence Inventory: A measure designed specifically for workplace applications. In Assessing Emotional Intelligence (pp. 103-117). Springer US.

16. Druskat, V. U., & Wolff, S. B. (2001). Building the emotional intelligence of groups. Harvard Business Review, 79(3), 80-91.

17. Hughes, M., & Terrell, J. B. (2011). The emotionally intelligent team: Understanding and developing the behaviors of success. John Wiley & Sons.

18. Hughes, M., & Terrell, J. B. (2011). The emotionally intelligent team: Understanding and developing the behaviors of success. John Wiley & Sons.

19. T., Tram, S., & O'Hara, L. A. (2006). Relation of employee and manager emotional intelligence to job satisfaction and performance. Journal of Vocational Behavior, 68(3), 461-473.

20. Nadler, R. S. (2011). Leading with emotional intelligence.

21. Caruso, D. R., Mayer, J. D., & Salovey, P. (2002). Emotional intelligence and emotional leadership. In *Kravis-de Roulet Leadership Conference, 9th, Apr, 1999,*

Claremont McKenna Coll, Claremont, CA, US. Lawrence Erlbaum Associates Publishers.

Chapter 8: The Psychology of Motivation

1. Maslow, A. H. (1943). A theory of human motivation. *Psychological Review, 50*(4), 370.
2. Thomas, K. W. (2000). Intrinsic motivation at work: Building energy & commitment. Berrett-Koehler Publishers.
3. Ryan, R. M., & Deci, E. L. (2000). Intrinsic and extrinsic motivations: Classic definitions and new directions. Contemporary educational psychology, 25(1), 54-67.
4. Ridgeway, C. L. (1982). Status in groups: The importance of motivation. American Sociological Review, 76-88.
5. Proudfit, G. H., Inzlicht, M., & Mennin, D. S. (2013). Anxiety and error monitoring: the importance of motivation and emotion. Frontiers in Human Neuroscience, 7, 636.
6. Henderson, M. C. (1995). Nurse executives: leadership motivation and leadership effectiveness. *Journal of Nursing Administration, 25*(4), 45-51.
7. Skinner, B. F. (1969). Contingencies of reinforcement: A theoretical analysis. New York: Appleton-Century-Crofts.
8. Eisenstadt, S. N. (1998). Japanese civilization: A comparative view. University of Chicago Press.
9. Harlow, H. F., Harlow, M. K., & Meyer, D.R. Learning motivated by a manipulation Drive. Journal of Experimental Psychology 40 (1950): 231

10. Deci, E. (1971). Effects of externally mediated rewards on intrinsic motivation. Journal of Personality and Social Psychology 18 (1971): 114.
11. Feller, J. (2005). Perspectives on free and open source software. Cambridge, Mass: MIT Press.
12. Kanfer, R., & Ackerman, P. L. (2004). Aging, adult development, and work motivation. Academy of Management Review, 29(3), 440-458.
13. The Fun Theory. (2009, September 21). Retrieved from http://www.thefuntheory.com/
14. Bradt, G. (2015, May 20). Disney's best ever example of motivating employees. Retrieved from http://www.forbes.com/sites/georgebradt/2015/05/20/disneys-best-ever-example-of-motivating-employees/#1011872ca648
15. Gast, I. M., & Skinner, H. C. (1929). Psychology of motivation. Fundamentals of Educational Psychology, 238-248.
16. Hackman, J. R., & Oldham, G. R. (1976). Motivation through the design of work: Test of a theory. Organizational Behavior and Human Performance,16(2), 250-279.
17. King, L. A. (2008). Personal goals and life dreams: Positive psychology and motivation in daily life. *Handbook of Motivation Science*, 518-530.
18. Perrin, F. A. C. (1923). The Psychology of motivation. Psychological Review, 30(3), 176.

19. Dweck, C. (2006). Mindset: The new psychology of success. Random House.
20. Cropanzano, R., James, K., & Citera, M. (1993). A goal hierarchy model of personality, motivation, and leadership. Research in Organizational Behavior, 15, 267-267.

Chapter 9: How to Use Psychology to enhance Goal Setting

1. Locke, E. A., Shaw, K. N., Saari, L. M., & Latham, G. P. (1981). Goal setting and task performance: 1969–1980. *Psychological bulletin*, *90*(1), 125.
2. Custers, R., & Aarts, H. (2005). Positive affect as implicit motivator: on the nonconscious operation of behavioral goals. Journal of Personality and Social Psychology, 89(2), 129.
3. House, R. J. (1971) A path goal theory of leader effectiveness. *Administrative Science Quarterly*, 321-339.
4. House, R. J. (1996). Path-goal theory of leadership: Lessons, legacy, and a reformulated theory. *The Leadership Quarterly*, 7(3), 323-352.
5. House, R. J. (1971). A path goal theory of leader effectiveness. Administrative Science Quarterly, 321-339.
6. House, R. J. (1971). A path goal theory of leader effectiveness. Administrative Science Quarterly, 321-339.
7. House, R. J. (1971). A path goal theory of leader effectiveness. Administrative Science Quarterly, 321-339.

8. House, R. J. (1971). A path goal theory of leader effectiveness. Administrative Science Quarterly, 321-339.
9. Ashkenas, R. (2012, July 09). Seven mistakes leaders make in setting goals. Retrieved from http://www.forbes.com/sites/ronashkenas/2012/07/09/seven-mistakes-leaders-make-in-setting-goals/#54e87bf4a0f3
10. Locke, E. A., Shaw, K. N., Saari, L. M., & Latham, G. P. (1981). Goal setting and task performance. Psychological Bulletin, 90, 125-152.
11. Brusso, R. C., Orvis, K. A., Bauer, K. N., & Tekleab, A. G. (2012). Interaction among self-efficacy, goal orientation, and unrealistic goal-setting on videogame-based training performance. Military Psychology, 24, 1-18.
12. Berry, J. M. & West, R. L. (1993). Cognitive self-efficacy in relation to personal mastery and goal setting across the lifespan. International Journal of Behavioral Development, 16(2), 351 - 379.
13. Frese, M., & Zapf, D. (1994). Action as the core of work psychology: A German approach. Handbook of Industrial and Organizational Psychology, volume 4 (2).
14. Mikulincer, M. (1988). Reactance and helplessness following exposure to unsolvable problems: The effects of attributional style. *Journal of Personality and Social Psychology*, 54, 679–686.

Chapter 10: How Psychology Can Help you Improve Productivity

1. Kirschbaum, C., Wolf, O. T., May, M., Wippich, W., & Hellhammer, D. H. (1996). Stress- and treatment-induced elevations of cortisol levels associated with impaired declarative memory in healthy adults. *Life Sciences, 58*(17), 1475-1483.
2. Rothblum, E. D. (1990). Fear of failure: The psychodynamic, need achievement, fear of success, and procrastination models. Handbook of Social and Evaluation Anxiety, 497-537.
3. Deloitte. (2014, October). The overwhelmed employee: Simplify the work environment. Global Research. Retrieved from https://www2.deloitte.com/au/en/pages/human-capital/articles/overwhelmed-employee-simplify-environment.html
4. Mischel, W., & Ebbesen, E. B. (1970). Attention in delay of gratification. *Journal of Personality and Social Psychology, 16*(2), 329.
5. Mischel, W., Shoda, Y., & Rodriguez, M. I. (1989). Delay of gratification in children. Science, 244(4907), 933-938.
6. Hamarta, E. (2014). An analysis of university students' interpersonal problem solving approaches with respect to their perfectionism. International Journal of Academic Research, 6(1).

7. Judge, T. A., & Bono, J. E. (2001). Relationship of core self-evaluations traits—self-esteem, generalized self-efficacy, locus of control, and emotional stability—with job satisfaction and job performance: A meta-analysis. Journal of Applied Psychology, 86(1), 80.
8. Covey, S. R. (1989). The 7 habits of highly effective people: Restoring the character ethic. Simon and Schuster.
9. Robbins, T. The power of chunking: Making more time for what really matters to you. (2013, March 13). Retrieved from https://training.tonyrobbins.com/how-to-turn-more-into-less-the-power-of-chunking/
10. Cirillo, F. (2006). The Pomodoro Technique (The Pomodoro). Agile Processes in Software Engineering and Extreme, 54(2).
11. Zeigarnik, B. (1927). On finished and unfinished tasks. *Psychologische Forschung, 9*.
12. Bandiera, O., Guison, L., Prat, A., & Sadun, R. (2011). *What do CEOs do?* Harvard Business School.
13. Heath, C., Larrick, R. P., & Wu, G. (1999). Goals as reference points. *Cognitive Psychology, 38*(1), 79-109.
14. Mager, R. F., & Pipe, P. (1970). Analyzing performance problems: or, "You really oughta wanna". Lake Publishers.
15. Allen, J., & Van der Velden, R. (2001). Educational mismatches versus skill mismatches: effects on wages, job satisfaction, and on-the-job search. *Oxford Economic Papers, 53*(3), 434-452.

Chapter 11: Using Psychology to Recruit Top Talent

1. Gillett, R. (2014). The staggering cost of a bad hire and how to avoid one. Retrieved from http://www.fastcompany.com/3028628/work-smart/infographic-how-much-a-bad-hire-will-actually-cost-you
2. Avoid these harmful hiring mistakes. (2013, June 28). Retrieved from http://www.forbes.com/sites/thesba/2013/06/28/avoid-these-harmful-hiring-mistakes/
3. Nisbett, R. E., & Wilson, T. D. (1977). The halo effect: Evidence for unconscious alteration of judgments. Journal of Personality and Social Psychology, 35(4), 250.
4. Landy, D., & Sigall, H. (1974). Beauty is talent: Task evaluation as a function of the performer's physical attractiveness. *Journal of Personality and Social Psychology, 29*(3), 299.
5. Robiner, W. N., Saltzman, S. R., Hoberman, H. M., Semrud-Clikeman, M., & Schirvar, J. A. (1998). Psychology supervisors' bias in evaluations and letters of recommendation. *The Clinical Supervisor, 16*, 49-72.
6. Brecher, E., Bragger, J., & Kutcher, E. (2006). The structured interview: Reducing biases toward job applicants with physical disabilities. *Employee Responsibilities and Rights Journal, 18*(3), 155-170.

7. Wason, P. C. (1960). On the failure to eliminate hypotheses in a conceptual task. *Quarterly journal of experimental psychology, 12*(3), 129-140.
8. Collisson, B., & Howell, J. L. (2014). The liking-similarity effect: Perceptions of similarity as a function of liking. *The Journal of Social Psychology, 154*(5), 384-400.
9. Asch, S. E. (1946). Forming impressions of personality. *The Journal of Abnormal and Social Psychology, 41*(3), 258.
10. Sherif, M., Taub, D., & Hovland, C. I. (1958). Assimilation and contrast effects of anchoring stimuli on judgments. *Journal of Experimental Psychology, 55*(2), 150.
11. Chapter 12: Using Psychology to Enhance Feedback
12. Ramaprasad, A. (1983). On the definition of feedback. *Behavioral Science, 28*(1), 4-13.
13. Bailey, J. R., Chen, C. C., & Dou, S. G. (1997). Conceptions of self and performance-related feedback in the US, Japan and China. *Journal of International Business Studies, 28*(3), 605-625.
14. London, M., Larsen, H. H., & Thisted, L. N. (1999). Relationships between feedback and self-development. *Group & Organization Management, 24*(1), 5-27.
15. Lepsinger, R., & Lucia, A. D. (2009). *The art and science of 360 degree feedback.* John Wiley & Sons.
16. Tziner, A., & Latham, G. P. (1989). The effects of appraisal instrument, feedback and goal-setting on worker

satisfaction and commitment. *Journal of Organizational Behavior, 10*(2), 145-153.

17. Dohrenwend, A. (2002). Serving up the feedback sandwich. *Family practice management, 9*(10), 43-50.

18. Gross, B. (2012, November 30). How to give great employee feedback. Retrieved from https://www.linkedin.com/pulse/20121130041419-9947747-how-to-give-great-employee-feedback

19. Archer, J. C. (2010). State of the science in health professional education: Effective feedback. *Medical Education, 44*(1), 101-108.

20. Schwarz, R. (2015, August 19). When to give feedback in a group and when to do it one-on-one. Retrieved from https://hbr.org/2015/08/when-to-give-feedback-in-a-group-and-when-to-do-it-one-on-one

21. Finkelstein, S. R., & Fishbach, A. (2012). Tell me what I did wrong: Experts seek and respond to negative feedback. *Journal of Consumer Research, 39*(1), 22-38.

22. Lepsinger, R., & Lucia, A. D. (2009). *The art and science of 360 degree feedback.* John Wiley & Sons.

23. Walker, A. G., & Smither, J. W. (1999). A five‐year study of upward feedback: What managers do with their results matters. Personnel Psychology, 52(2), 393-423.

24. Stone, D., & Heen, S. (2015). Thanks for the feedback: The science and art of receiving feedback well. Penguin.

25. Langer, E. J., Blank, A., & Chanowitz, B. (1978). The mindlessness of ostensibly thoughtful action: The role of "placebic" information in interpersonal interaction. *Journal of Personality and Social Psychology, 36*(6), 635.

Chapter 13: Using Psychology to Handle Conflict and Deal with Difficult People

1. Heitler, S. (1990). From conflict to resolution. *M. Isenhart and M. Spangle, Collaborative Approaches to Resolving Conflict, Thousand Oaks, CA: Sage Publications.*
2. Allen, B. (n.d.). Conflict Resolution Management.
3. Goodwin, D. K. (2009). Team of rivals: The political genius of Abraham Lincoln. Penguin UK.
4. Stein, K. W. (1999). Heroic diplomacy: Sadat, Kissinger, Carter, Begin, and the quest for Arab-Israeli peace. Psychology Press.
5. Fisher, R., & Ury, W. (1987). Getting to yes. Simon & Schuster Sound Ideas.
6. Fisher, R. J. (1990). Needs theory, social identity and an eclectic model of conflict. In Conflict: Human Needs Theory (pp. 89-112). Palgrave Macmillan UK.
7. Galtung, J. (2000). Conflict transformation by peaceful means: The transcend method. UN.
8. Maravelas, A. (2005). How to reduce workplace conflict and stress: How leaders and their employees can protect

their sanity and productivity from tension and turf wars. Career Press.

9. The Betari Box. (n.d.). Retrieved from http://changingminds.org/explanations/behaviors/betari_box.htm

10. Fisher, S. (2000). *Working with conflict: skills and strategies for action*. Zed books.

11. Mohr, J., & Spekman, R. (1994). Characteristics of partnership success: partnership attributes, communication behavior, and conflict resolution techniques. *Strategic Management Journal*, *15*(2), 135-152.

12. Bolton, R. (2009). *People skills*. Simon and Schuster.

Chapter 14: The Psychology of Teams

1. Teamwork. (n.d.). Retrieved from http://www.psychologyandsociety.com/teamwork.html

2. Hoegl, M., Parboteeah, K. P., & Gemuenden, H. G. (2003). When teamwork really matters: Task innovativeness as a moderator of the teamwork–performance relationship in software development projects. Journal of Engineering and Technology Management, 20(4), 281-302.

3. Morey, J. C., Simon, R., Jay, G. D., Wears, R. L., Salisbury, M., Dukes, K. A., & Berns, S. D. (2002). Error reduction and performance improvement in the emergency department through formal teamwork training: Evaluation results of the MedTeams project. Health Services Research, 37(6), 1553-1581.

4. Orsburn, J. D. (1996). Self-directed work teams: The new American challenge. Irwin Professional Pub.
5. Curşeu, P. L., & Pluut, H. (2013). Student groups as learning entities: The effect of group diversity and teamwork quality on groups' cognitive complexity. Studies in Higher Education, 38(1), 87-103.
6. Palfini, J. (2008, June 17). Four great teams in business istory. Retrieved from http://www.cbsnews.com/news/four-great-teams-in-business-history/
7. Peteraf, M., & Shanley, M. (1997). Getting to know you: A theory of strategic group identity. Strategic Management Journal, 18, 165-186. Retrieved from http://www.jstor.org/stable/3088215
8. Costa, A. C. (2003). Work team trust and effectiveness. Personnel Review, 32(5), 605-622.
9. Bradley, J. H., & Hebert, F. J. (1997). The effect of personality type on team performance. *Journal of Management Development, 16*(5), 337-353.
10. Woolley, A. W., Chabris, C. F., Pentland, A., Hashmi, N., & Malone, T. W. (2010). Evidence for a collective intelligence factor in the performance of human groups. *Science, 330*(6004), 686-688.
11. Lyttle, J. (2007). The judicious use and management of humor in the workplace. *Business Horizons, 50*(3), 239-245.

12. Westli, H. K., Johnsen, B. H., Eid, J., Rasten, I., & Brattebø, G. (2010). Teamwork skills, shared mental models, and performance in simulated trauma teams: An independent group design. *Scandinavian Journal of Trauma, Resuscitation and Emergency Medicine*, 18(1), 1.
13. Lencioni, P. M. (2002). *The five dysfunctions of a team: A leadership fable* (Vol. 13). John Wiley & Sons.

Chapter 15: Using Psychology to Influence Culture

1. Organizational Culture. (n.d.). Retrieved from http://www.psychologyandsociety.com/organizationalculture.html
2. Patel, S. (2015, August 6). 10 examples of companies with fantastic cultures. Retrieved from https://www.entrepreneur.com/article/249174
3. Gordon, G. G., & DiTomaso, N. (1992). Predicting corporate performance from organizational culture. Journal of Management Studies, 29(6), 783-798.
4. Buligo, Z. (2013) Tony Hsieh, Zappos, and the art of great company culture. Retrieved from https://blog.kissmetrics.com/zappos-art-of-culture/
5. About Zappos culture. (n.d.). Retrieved from http://www.zappos.com/core-values
6. Stephens, G.R. (1965, January). Cultural acquisition of a specific learned response among rhesus monkeys.

In American Zoologist (Vol. 5, No. 4, p. 677). 1041 New Hampshire St, Lawrence, KS 66044: American Society of Zoologists.
7. The famous 'social experiment': 5 monkeys and a ladder. (2014, May 28). Retrieved from http://www.wisdompills.com/2014/05/28/the-famous-social-experiment-5-monkeys-a-ladder/
8. Barney, J. B. (1986). Organizational culture: Can it be a source of sustained competitive advantage?. Academy of Management review, 11(3), 656-665.
9. O'Reilly, C. A., Chatman, J., & Caldwell, D. F. (1991). People and organizational culture: A profile comparison approach to assessing person-organization fit. *Academy of Management Journal*, 34(3), 487-516.
10. Weick, K. E. (1987). Organizational culture as a source of high reliability. *California Management Review*, 29(2), 112-127.

Chapter 16: The Psychology of Change

1. Jacobson, N. S., & Truax, P. (1991). Clinical significance: A statistical approach to defining meaningful change in psychotherapy research. *Journal of Consulting and Clinical Psychology*, 59(1), 12.
2. Ridley, M. (2015). The evolution of everything: How ideas emerge. HarperCollins UK.

3. Faeste, L., Hemerling, J., Keenan, P., & Reeves, M. (2014, November 3). Five case studies of transformation excellence. Retrieved from https://www.bcgperspectives.com/content/articles/transformation_change_management_five_case_studies_transformation_excellence/
4. Goleman, D. (1998). The emotional intelligence of leaders. Leader to Leader, 1998 (10), 20-26.
5. Eagleman, D. (2015). The brain: The story of you. Pantheon.
6. Yin, H. H., & Knowlton, B. J. (2006). The role of the basal ganglia in habit formation. Nature Reviews Neuroscience, 7(6), 464-476.
7. Rock, D. (2008). SCARF: A brain-based model for collaborating with and influencing others. NeuroLeadership Journal, 1(1), 44-52.
8. Eisenberger, N. I., Lieberman, M. D., & Williams, K. D. (2003). Does rejection hurt? An fMRI study of social exclusion. Science, 302(5643), 290-292.
9. Hedden, T., & Gabrieli, J. D. (2006). The ebb and flow of attention in the human brain. *Nature Neuroscience*, 9(7), 863-865.
10. Rodin, J. (1986). Aging and health: Effects of the sense of control. *Science*, 233(4770), 1271-1276.
11. Carter, E. J., & Pelphrey, K. A. (2008). Friend or foe? Brain systems involved in the perception of dynamic

signals of menacing and friendly social approaches. *Social Neuroscience*, 3(2), 151-163.
12. Tabibnia, G., & Lieberman, M. D. (2007). Fairness and cooperation are rewarding. *Annals of the New York Academy of Sciences*, 1118(1), 90-101.
13. Festinger, L. (1962). *A theory of cognitive dissonance (Vol. 2)*. Stanford University Press.
14. Skinner, B. F. (1958). Reinforcement today. *American Psychologist*, 13(3), 94.
15. Goldberg, S. (2002, September 01). The 10 rules of change. Retrieved from https://www.psychologytoday.com/articles/200209/the-10-rules-change
16. Rock, D., & Donde, R. (2008). Driving organizational change with internal coaching programs: Part one. *Industrial and Commercial Training*, 40(1), 10-18.
17. Simons, D. J., & Levin, D. T. (1997). Change blindness. *Trends in Cognitive Sciences*, 1(7), 261-267.

Chapter 17: The Psychology of Millennials

1. Howe, N., & Strauss, W. (1992). *Generations: The history of America's future, 1584 to 2069*. Harper Collins.
2. Hershatter, A., & Epstein, M. (2010). Millennials and the world of work: An organization and management perspective. Journal of Business and Psychology, 25(2), 211-223.

3. Ng, E., Lyons, S. T., & Schweitzer, L. (Eds.). (2012). Managing the new workforce: International perspectives on the millennial generation. Edward Elgar Publishing.
4. Myers, K. K., & Sadaghiani, K. (2010). Millennials in the workplace: A communication perspective on millennials' organizational relationships and performance. *Journal of Business and Psychology*, 25(2), 225-238.
5. Deal, J. J., Altman, D. G., & Rogelberg, S. G. (2010). Millennials at work: What we know and what we need to do (if anything). Journal of Business and Psychology, 25(2), 191-199.
6. Trzesniewski, K. H., & Donnellan, M. B. (2010). Rethinking "generation me": A study of cohort effects from 1976–2006. Perspectives on Psychological Science, 5(1) 58–75.
7. Ng, E. S., Schweitzer, L., & Lyons, S. T. (2010). New generation, great expectations: A field study of the millennial generation. Journal of Business and Psychology, 25(2), 281-292.
8. De Hauw, S., & De Vos, A. (2010). Millennials' career perspective and psychological contract expectations: does the recession lead to lowered expectations? *Journal of Business and Psychology*, 25(2), 293-302.
9. Hershatter, A., & Epstein, M. (2010). Millennials and the world of work: An organization and management perspective. *Journal of Business and Psychology*, 25(2), 211-223.

10. Pew Research Center. Retrieved from http://www.pewresearch.org/topics/millennials/
11. SmithBucklin (2017). Retrieved from http://www.smithbucklin.com/news/millennials-can-add-unique-value-to-the-boardroom/
12. Deal, J. J., Altman, D. G., & Rogelberg, S. G. (2010). Millennials at work: What we know and what we need to do (if anything). *Journal of Business and Psychology, 25*(2), 191-199.
13. Ferri-Reed, J. (2010). The keys to engaging millennials. *The Journal for Quality and Participation, 33*(1), 31.
14. Kowske, B. J., Rasch, R., & Wiley, J. (2010). Millennials' (lack of) attitude problem: An empirical examination of generational effects on work attitudes. *Journal of Business and Psychology, 25*(2), 265-279.
15. Generations in the workplace: Winning the generation game. Retrieved from http://www.economist.com/news/business/21586831-businesses-are-worrying-about-how-manage-different-age-groups-widely-different
16. Alexander, C. S., & Sysko, J. M. (2011, January). A study of the cognitive determinants of generation y's entitlement mentality. In *Allied Academies International Conference. Academy of Educational Leadership. Proceedings, 16*(1), 1. Jordan Whitney Enterprises, Inc.

17. Dorsey, J. R. (2009). *Y-size your business: How Gen Y employees can save you money and grow your business.* John Wiley & Sons.
18. Brack, J. (2012). Maximizing Millennials in the workplace. *UNC Executive Development,* 1-14.
19. The millennial generation research review. (2012, November 12). Retrieved from https://www.uschamberfoundation.org/reports/millennial-generation-research-review
20. Mencl, J. & Lester, S.W. (2014). More alike than different: What generations value and how the values affect employee workplace perceptions. *Journal of Leadership and Organizational Studies, 21*(3).
21. Peters, S. (2012, February 08). How GE is attracting, developing, and retaining global talent. Retrieved from https://hbr.org/2012/02/how-ge-is-attracting-and-devel
22. Kossek, E. E., & Lee, M. D. (2008). Implementing a reduced-workload arrangement to retain high talent: A case study. *The Psychologist-Manager Journal, 11*(1), 49-64.

Felicia Page
MOrgPsych, BSc (Psychology with Honours), Cert IV Training and Assessment

Felicia Page is an Organizational Psychologist and Global Coaching and Leadership Development Specialist. Felicia works with CEOs, Executives and Entrepreneurs to gain competitive advantage through people.

Felicia has proven success in leading Organizational Development in large, medium and small entities, in diverse global organizations, and across a range of industries including Health, IT, Professional Services, Education, Mining, Science, Government and Private Sector. A sample of these organizations include BHP Billiton, Collins Foods, The Department of Environment and Heritage Protection, Air Niugini, and Trade and Investment Queensland.

Felicia Page - The back story

Described by her peers as having great passion, enthusiasm and natural flair, Felicia spent her early years observing people and the dynamics of interactions. She began to recognise that the way we engage with people determines our success or failure in every endeavour. When she started her career in Psychology, she was fascinated to see how small changes in employee behaviour and mindset could affect the outcome for an entire organization.

Now, Felicia accelerates people performance for leaders and organizations who are ready to hear what they need to hear rather than what they want to hear.

Outside of the workplace, you will find Felicia hiking with her dog, defending on the netball court or Watching Shark Tank.